KILL

THE

STUPID

AND OTHER

MUSINGS

THE FULL BOOK

BY

JIM MACIVER

Dedication

This book is dedicated to the future generation that will know I was right all along.

Table of Contents

Introduction to the New Edition

This tome is the full-size book I promised when I released my "mini-book." When I released the first edition of *Kill the Stupid,* it was with the intention to get it out quickly. I didn't think Donald Trump would be president very long. I thought Robert Mueller would have taken him down by now, or Trump would just resign because he couldn't take the pressure of the job. I see now how wrong I was to expect a quick conclusion to Mueller's investigation. Going after a president of the United States, even one so obviously corrupt as Donald Trump takes time. Every i must be dotted, and every t must be crossed. This is especially true since the president is accused of conspiracy and possibly treason. I've lost hope he will resign unless he is forced to do so by the threat of prosecution. It turns out Donald Trump likes being president. He can steal from and oppress people on a grand scale far in excess from what he could do as a mere real estate mogul with probable Mafia ties.

I also wanted to give more insight and clarification into the views I expressed in the first edition. This edition is longer and covers a wider variety of subjects. Again, none of these essays explore in great depth. That is what books are for.

These essays are intended to give you some superficial knowledge to provide you with a starting point. I hope you might come to advocate for some of the proposals which I have made. I know some of them are controversial. Times change. There was once a time when people believed (and some still do) the Earth is flat. Positive change can occur, but only if people commit to that accomplishment.

As before, I have made extensive use of various sources, including Wikipedia and Buzzfeed. When I have quoted a book or a significant idea, I cited those sources as well. However, this is not a scholarly piece. As before, I strongly advise you to check for yourselves.

I do not think of myself as a public intellectual or anything like that. I'm probably not the best writer, either. I'm just a regular guy who thinks he has some good ideas. I needed to express them in the forum of public discourse. Ultimately, it is you who will decide if this work has any merit or not. The fact you even are reading this book demonstrates you have a concern for humanity and are willing to explore different options for making the world a better place, even if they are not of the conventional wisdom. Welcome to my world and my view of it. Hopefully, you will discover it is a vision you wish to share.

Introduction

In the beginning,.... was this introduction. The United States, and probably the world as well, needs a new direction. Hopefully, this short missive will provide it or at least give useful suggestions toward making that new world.

Originally this was intended as one of my Facebook rants on what I consider the two biggest dangers to the planet, overpopulation, and religion. I say this because both lead to climate change, hunger, poverty, crime, pollution, sometimes war, and most of humanity's other problems.

As I was writing, I realized I could not merely opine about these two issues. Many causes have brought overpopulation and religious abuse, and they need to be addressed as well. Politics, the greed of huge corporations, anti-science, and general human ignorance, are contributing factors.

My approach to problems has always been to eliminate them. To me, this seems the logical approach to these kinds of issues. I think for too long, we have thought we could "fix" our difficulties by throwing money at them or, in the case of specific people problems, coddling them in the hopes they will do better. It is a waste of time and resources to do this. Even our enemies know this.

Our "enemies" you ask? Who are they? They are the religionists, the money-hungry people who run the large corporations, the Owners as I call them (after the great George Carlin) the politicians in their pockets, the abusers of power and racists and other haters. You have probably realized I am an Atheist/Humanist, or a Humanist/Atheist. It is my nature to want to help my fellow human beings.

In response, I have written this book. You might even call it a manifesto. It seemed to me this was something I needed to get out quickly so we could start fighting right away. Even so, although I want you to agree with me and maybe start a movement, I did not want to write a book where I spoon-fed you all the information, though I have expanded it into a full volume. I want you to do research on your own, find the facts for yourselves, and reach your own conclusions. To that end, I decided to keep this short. It does not cover all the subjects I'd like it to, but there is always the future. Many of these essays are less than five pages long and do not need to be read in any particular order. I also wanted to have this be a size you could carry with you easily. I grew up in the era of books, not Kindles, so this was part of my motivation. Lastly, I want this to be sold at a price everyone could afford. Let's face it; you're not going to have a lot of disposable income now that Donald Trump is president.

I will spell out our problems as I see them and will offer suggestions on how to address them. You may not agree with them. You may want to burn this book and me along with it. That's ok so long as it gets you thinking. I am sure there are others, some of my personal acquaintance, who could express these thoughts much better than I. The problem is I don't see any of them writing this book.

We have a significant problem right now. We have a thin-skinned, psychotic president with the temperament of a two-year-old. He whines and cries every time he doesn't get his way. He thinks he can run the country as if it were a business and bully other countries. He has only been in office for a few months (as of this writing) and has already damaged the country in the eyes of the world. Maybe he is not concerned about that because he plans to take the world over? I don't know. I just know he needs to be stopped and put on trial. While we're at it, we should put every president since Jimmy Carter on trial too. Carter was a good man, although he was somewhat incompetent on some things. However, he was sincere and became more presidential after he left office. Those who followed him were all obligated to the Owners. They waged wars for profit and allowed corporations to have even more control of our country. They must be punished for what they have done.

We also have a greedy Congress bought and paid for by the Owners. We need to take them all down. I don't want to overthrow the United States, but I do want to defeat these criminals who have taken over. Pull them all out of office and subject them to trial. Those who have worked for the people will be welcomed back to their offices. Those who have worked against the people will be permanently removed.

I want to take this country back. I also want to take this country forward. I want to destroy the destructive influence of the Owners and the religious cults. This book will not have every strategy worked out or every move planned. That is what I'm counting on you folks for. Ultimately it is you, me, WE that will save the planet and our democracy.

While this slim volume is an opinion piece, it is my sincere hope my little book can help bring about a more peaceful, logical world. To get to that world, I see a long, complicated, and sometimes violent road ahead. We must become warriors in the fight against bigotry and hatred, ignorance, greed, corruption, and, even though I know, it is only a personification, evil.

Kill the Stupid

As we all know, there are many problems in our current world. It is so overwhelming; one hardly knows where to begin. Climate change, corporate greed, the downfall of the United States, terrorism, the wholesale murder of citizens by police, particularly black youth, income inequality, the dumbing down of society, the desperate and dangerous religious cults, the poisoning of our water and air, massive corruption, war and the constant threat of war. What do we do? How can we fix this?

"This planet might be able to support perhaps as many as half a billion people who could live a sustainable life in relative comfort. Human populations must be greatly diminished, and as quickly as possible to limit further environmental damage." – Biologist Eric Pianka

There is a way. However, it is a way that will call for total commitment. It is a way that is not politically correct. It will call for offending sensibilities, including our own—the trampling of human rights. We might feel terrible about doing it. In the end, it is what must be done. Sometimes, the end *does* justify the means.

I doubt it even can be accomplished. There are many, perhaps even myself, who will want to oppose this. In any case, we must overcome such considerations. We must do what is right and logical to preserve our species. If we don't, we will all die. Depending on which method we use, the world will improve in as little as twenty years or as many as eighty to one hundred years. It just depends on what we are willing to do to create a better world if we are eager to prolong our suffering for kindness sake and what we are willing to live with.

When you add up all our problems, they are caused, directly or indirectly, by the massive overpopulation on this planet. The obvious solution is to reduce the population. That sounds simple enough, but how do you do it? That is the question that haunts those who are engaged in finding a solution. I think I have the answer. To most, it will seem draconian and cruel. Still, I see no other way out of this since we do not yet possess the technology to terraform Mars or anyplace else, never mind the ability to transport a large portion of the population there. Even if we did, it would be a stop-gap measure, not a permanent solution.

We must reduce our population. How do we do that? How do we stop the world population growing past the point the planet can no longer sustain life on the earth? Remember, it is not just human life but also animal life and plant life. So, what do we do? We could all accept things as they are, a growing population that will end life on Earth long before we can get a handle on it. Why? Because somehow people have determined human life is somehow "sacred" even though nature does not recognize any such privileged status for human beings or anything else. Human beings do not recognize this so-called fact either. We have all sorts of justifications to exterminate our fellow humans. Why can't we add one more? Let's add a reason that will truly make sense and improve our lives.

In short, we need to eliminate at least two-thirds of the population. This idea will not be popular, which I'm sure will be the understatement of the year. Many will be opposed to this. The large corporations, which depend on an ever-expanding base of consumers and workers that they can keep needy and desperate, will fight this viciously. This solution will also be opposed by the religious cults, each of which seeks to control the world with a strategy of outbreeding all the others. Think of the "Quiverfull" movement supported by the over-breeding Duggar family. They like to think of themselves following their god's command to "be fruitful and multiply," Most religions have some form of this idea. Lastly, objection will come from ordinary people. No one wants to see innocent people suffer for things they are not responsible for. The sad thing is, they are already.

Ok, so let's say we all agree X number of people need to die. Who do we exterminate? In the Dan Brown novel *Inferno*, a scientist plans (apparently, but not really) to release a plague to kill one-third of the population. Just kill them with no distinction. Eric Pianka suggested the same thing, only using the Ebola virus. How is that supposed to work? The survivors, following the edicts of both the corporate masters and their Bibles, will go about replacing the deceased with brand new eaters who will swell the population back up. In just a few years we will be right back where we started.

This sort of approach makes no sense. Randomly killing human beings won't work. The right people must be selected to die. You also need to modify behavior as well, so you won't have to do this every few years and, hopefully, never again. What this comes down to is the people not chosen to die must be intelligent and logical. As you might expect, this brings us to the non-intelligent and illogical. In other words, the stupid.

So, what determines stupid? Most of us would say that is obvious; people who cannot get your order straight in a fast food restaurant, cannot learn something after repeated instruction or simply repeatedly make bad life choices like having children they cannot afford. We must remember there may be extenuating circumstances in these situations. Let me be clear. I do not wish to include those who suffer from a mental handicap since their condition is not their fault. I suggest we create IQ tests that will accurately measure human intelligence and make our determinations based on these tests.

Despite their sad purpose, these tests will yield positive results. We will no doubt find people who are intelligent but were ignored for whatever reason. For these people, we will bring up their education level, making them more productive to society. Of course, we will mainly find those who never bothered to learn because of either laziness or a conscious decision not to learn. I call them stupid and proud of it people. They are those who possess no critical thinking skills, who blindly follow so-called leaders (often as foolish and dim-witted as themselves) and partake in tribalism, the leading cause of racism. These people, and more importantly, these attitudes need to be stamped out.

Next, we will turn our attention to the willfully ignorant, an extension of those who made the conscious decision not to learn. This group will encompass all religious people. These people possess average intelligence (more or less) but allow themselves to buy into the delusion of god belief. They have held humanity back for centuries. Another form of tribalism, the religious try to entice or force you to join their tribe—all for something they cannot provide one iota of evidence. Nearly every day, we learn of some new atrocity by religionists. From the two women who gouged their sister's eyes out because they thought she was possessed to the woman who shot her friend who did not believe in God to the Christian terrorist who shot up a Planned Parenthood clinic. Add this to the murders committed by Muslims, Jews, and other cults, and you have a preponderance of what could be legitimately called evil.

Speaking of evil, another way of reducing the population is by executing all prisoners. Excepting those who are awaiting trial, we could clear out the prisons then convert them to better uses like homeless shelters, hospitals, schools, and the like. First, we must perform DNA and whatever other tests to determine guilt or innocence. Too often, people get railroaded into prison. People of color feel this oppression, particularly. These tests will free many. Those whose tests are inconclusive will return to their cells. Those who are guilty will be immediately executed.

Next, we will explore a way we could avoid the drastic methods I have just described. They won't be as efficient as the above methods but might seem more palpable to the average person. This way will take more time to deliver results, perhaps one hundred years or more, and will require a total commitment from society to sustain this plan.

An essential part of this plan is to re-visit the practice of Eugenics. For those unfamiliar with the term, it is similar to animal husbandry but applied to humans. Eugenics proposed we could better the species through selective breeding to create superior human beings. It also involves the sterilization of those deemed inferior. This idea seemed reasonable enough, but unfortunately, any time humans are concerned, there is always a danger of things going wrong. Eugenics was cursed by the prejudices of the people who were its most influential advocates. Eugenics was plagued by charges of racism, which were sadly true. It did not help that the Nazis adopted a form of Eugenics during World War II. Who was to be sterilized was being judged based on visions of white superiority instead of reason, logic, and science. Therefore, a great idea that could have saved us from the nightmare of over-population was discarded.

The time has come to revive Eugenics. This time, the bigotry that became inherent in Eugenics will be removed. Decisions concerning sterilization shall be made via computers with input from the IQ tests, as mentioned earlier. In this plan, no one will be killed. We will merely be assisting in the die-off of less functioning humans. You could think of it as actively taking control of our evolution.

We can also increase women's rights (by making them equal to men's rights) and women's options. This course has been shown to reduce the population by merely allowing women to be more than baby machines. A rewarding career and making a real contribution to humanity is far more fulfilling than popping out children.

There are other things we can do, as well. Make suicide legal and painless in all 50 states and territories. People should be able to end their lives for any reason they see fit. Let them meet with a psychologist first to see if they are sound of mind and, if so, proceed. Fully fund and promote abortion through positive ad campaigns and reinforcement from doctors, sports figures, anyone the public respects. We can also make abortion mandatory for people who are drug addicts, cannot afford to have children, those who do not have a committed partner, or are just plain irresponsible. Make sterilization (for both boys and girls) a happy event. Have parties and the like to make sterilization a family celebration. Perhaps we could call them Free Life Celebrations. Show the misery caused by having a large family or any family at all. These procedures should remain in effect even after population reduction is achieved to help maintain a healthy sized population.

I know this is a hard pill to swallow, but it must be done. I know this will be hard both emotionally and as a practical matter. No one wants to see people they know, even perhaps friends and family members, be put to death or allowed to die out. I wouldn't either. However, we must consider the greater good. They will be dark times, but like the person emerging from a long dark tunnel, we will find ourselves enveloped by the brightness and warmth of the sun. The new world order will greet us.

UPDATE: While I still consider overpopulation to be extremely dangerous, I see now the stupid are a reason unto themselves to justify their extermination. As I will explain in the following chapter, the stupid's very existence endangers civilization.

Ten Reasons Why We Must Kill the Stupid

In the previous essay, I suggested we need to kill the stupid. Although I thought the reasons were obvious, many have disagreed with me. It is true I was more focused on the mechanics than the why. Also, when I wrote it, I was more concerned about overpopulation. I have since realized that even if overpopulation were not a concern, this would still need to be done. Therefore, I see now a more detailed explanation is in order. I will explain things as I see them. These are not in any particular order since what I consider necessary may not be what you consider important. I think I have covered everything, but if any of you have additional reasons, please let me know.

The stupid hold us back: Human history is the story of human achievement. We started at the point in the distant past where we knew absolutely nothing. We began to learn. First, we discovered fire. Then we learned to create fire ourselves. We hunted with rocks, then with spears, and later with the bow and arrow. We taught ourselves how to till the land and grow food in addition to hunting and gathering.

Next, we moved on to form societies beyond the simple tribal form we had previously lived in.

Human beings began to specialize. We selected leaders. In time we formed governments and philosophies. We observed the world around us, from which came science. Our simple cave paintings became art. We developed healthcare and medicine. History has been a continuous line of achievement from the dawn of humanity to the modern age.

However, this progress has not been a smooth ride. We have had hiccups along the way. Throughout history, the ignorant have held back growth. There have been several reasons for this. Among these reasons have been superstition, bigotry, and fear, fear of the unknown, fear of change. Some have speculated if civilization had not been held back, we would be anywhere from 200 to 1000 years more advanced than we are now. The number can be debated, of course, but there is no doubt in my mind the human race would be more advanced than it is now.

The stupid take us to war: To be fair, this is something that cannot be entirely laid at the feet of the stupid. Many factors contribute to conflict. Social, economic, religious, the coveting of land, or only the desire for conquest. However. Sometimes a war might start over something we might consider insane. In the novel, *Gulliver's Travels* by Jonathan Swift, the nations of Lilliput and Blefuscu are fighting a bitter war. The war originated from a disagreement over the proper end to crack open a hard-boiled egg. While this is satire, wars have started over such silly reasons.

In 1828, angry mobs spurred on by a military coup destroyed a pastry shop owned by an expatriate French baker named Remontel. When Mexico ignored his requests for compensation, Remontel wrote to officials in France. Also ignored by France for a decade, it came to the attention of King Louis-Phillippe. The king (already angry over unpaid loans Mexico owed) demanded Mexico pay 600,000 pesos to Remontel. When Mexico refused, Louis-Phillippe sent a fleet of ships to shell the San Juan de Ulua Citadel. The British eventually negotiated a peace treaty. A condition of which was Mexico had to pay the 600,000 pesos. Sadly enough. This story is not the only example of this. Thanks to History.com. for their help.

The stupid are easily manipulated: One can look at any period of history to find examples of this. In our case, all we need to do is look at a newspaper or watch the news. Although the news media also manipulates people, the most glaring example comes from politics. One politician, in particular, you call him Mr. President. Trump is a master at manipulating his followers. They believe anything he tells them and refuses to acknowledge information that contradicts him. All Trump has to say are the magic words, "FAKE NEWS!" and his moronic base believes all news is fake. The news media is not false; although it is true, they can slant stories to their narrative.

When Kellyanne Conway, Counselor to the President and Head Minister of Propaganda, declared the existence of "alternative facts," Trump's mindless minions swooned. The stupid has no use for facts or, for that matter, reality itself. They live in a perpetual limbo of fantasy and denial. They do not confirm what they hear with multiple sources. They do not check facts because, as previously stated, they do not believe in facts. Everything for them is based on emotion. How they feel is what is important to them. Any good manipulator knows this. Therefore, Trump loves the "poorly educated." Because of this:

The stupid are not good citizens: This is why I have suggested we test voters. Very often, people are swayed by advertising and celebrity. This tendency is especially true with Donald Trump but applies across the board. Many of those "smart enough" to oppose Trump were ecstatic over the possibility that Oprah Winfrey, another TV personality, might run for office. The mindset seems to be "He/she is on television! He/she must be the best for the job!" It appears that in our media-obsessed culture, competence is equated with television exposure.

The Founders would have been horrified by this way of thinking. They knew an educated electorate was essential to preserve freedom. Jefferson said ". . . whenever the people are well-informed, they can be trusted with their own government; that, whenever things get so far wrong as to attract their notice, they may be relied on to set them right." In my view, not to be educated about those you vote for is not only ignorance and laziness. It is a form of treason. It says you are willing to allow your country to fall apart because you could not be bothered to learn anything about those for whom you voted—those who will make decisions that affect your life and the lives of your fellow citizens.

The stupid believe in fairy tales and other nonsense: From the beginnings of human history, our species has sought to understand the world. The world was complicated. Its workings are a mystery. Since it was difficult for them to comprehend, they concluded something greater than themselves must be in control. From this idea came the gods. They are found in every culture. The whole concept is based on a convoluted logic. You see a chair; someone must have made it. You see a house; someone must have built it. You know the world; someone must have created it.

Our current problems began in the Bronze Age. This era was when ancient goat herders in northern Africa created their god. The world has been miserable ever since. Throughout the centuries, the religious expanded their myths. After the original stories featuring Moses (Charlton Heston), new legends were added around a character named Jesus. Jesus, aka Yeshua, was based on various savior myths from earlier times, such as Osiris and Mithra. He never existed. There is not a single contemporary account of the man, although, according to the New Testament, he was a rock star in his day. Next came Mohammed, the founder of Islam. Unlike Jesus, he did have the advantage of actually existing. He lived from 570 CE-632 CE. He was considered a prophet as opposed to a god-thing but has still been the cause of violent history.

The problem with believing in a god is you have to figure out what he or she wants. To begin with, how do we even know what the god's gender is? Would it also have a gender? Don't worry, some folks interpret all that for you and answer your questions. They call themselves priests, rabbis, imams, ministers, preachers, and so on. There is no shortage of titles they give themselves. They all claim to be in direct communication with their god. I suppose they have his speed dial.

Since people trust these so-called leaders to interpret their god-thing's wishes, these interpreters can say and get people to do anything they want. This thought process would include getting followers to do their bidding, either in a sexual context or more violent activities. How many suicide bombers or shooters have been "inspired" to perpetuate these horrors? Voltaire said: "Those who can make you believe absurdities can make you commit atrocities." He is proven correct nearly every single day.

Of course, religion does not have to be violent to be destructive. Religionists engage in their destructiveness every day. They do it in overt ways, such as promoting Creationism and influencing lawmakers to favor their religious cult despite the Constitutional provision against it or actively attempting to overthrow the government to install a theocracy. They do it in more subtle ways like discrimination against others, not of their religion, politics, sex, or sexual orientation. People allow themselves to be conned by televangelists offering fake cures.

Not all the nonsense people believe in is religious. Look at all the people who believe in various forms of supernaturalism. How many follow psychics? How many follow their horoscopes? How many carry rabbits' feet?

What this all comes down to is people are basing their lives on mythology and superstition. There are no gods. This time is the 21st Century, yet too many humans still believe the musings of ancient goat herders and other assorted nonsense.

The stupid denies science and facts: If you have ever discussed science and/or events with stupid people, you probably found they lacked in understanding. You may have even seen them in denial of reality. Facts are hard things to understand for many people. They cannot comprehend facts are objective as opposed to subjective. They think facts are something that is made up, especially by people they don't like.

Look at Creationism. Now, this is something that is made up. Creationism, also known as Intelligent Design, is a response to Darwin's theory of evolution. Evolution is the lynchpin of our understanding of biology. Creationism is the denial of biological science in favor of religious myth. Its proponents, which include Vice-President Mike Pence, want to replace science with Creationism or, as they put it, "teach the controversy." The truth is, there is no controversy. Evolution is settled science. The only conflicts involve mechanisms. That is the nature of science. Theories are retested continuously. The more researchers try to disprove evolution and fail, the more confidence they can have in it.

Perhaps that is what frightens opposers of evolution. Of course, there are their cult beliefs. Could it also be the constantly changing nature of science scares them? Science is in continual flux. With religion, learning is just a one and done sort of thing. "God did it!" There is nothing else you need to learn. That seems to be a comfort to them. It is just fear.

Let's look at another idea that is settled science. The concept that the Earth is round. As you may have heard, the view of a flat Earth is coming back. Some people insist the Earth is flat even though we have known it is round since the 3rd Century BCE. In their reality, Earth is pictured as a disc, or sometimes as an upside-down mountain. They claim there is a wall of ice along the edge (so the people don't fall off or the water spill out, silly!) However; no one has ever been to this ice wall. The reason is that it is guarded by government agents who have protected this secret since, I guess, the dawn of time. Flat Earthers also don't care much for the Copernican Heliocentric theory, either. They think the sun hovers above the Earth, moving back and forth to create day and night. Moreover, Flat Earthers don't accept Isaac Newton's theory of gravity (what did he know?) Flat Earthers subscribe to their own version, Universal Acceleration, which posits there is a force underneath the Earth that perpetually pushes it upward. There is a second version that involves dark energy.

When I first heard of the Flat Earth Society, I thought it was meant to be a satiric joke. If I didn't already know about them, I would have assumed the same for Creationism. They are both attacks on science to advance stupidity. A world so dependent on science cannot allow such nonsense to continue unless their adherents do one thing: PROVE IT!

The stupid breed like rabbits: The original impetus for writing *Kill the Stupid* came from a concern for over-population. My thoughts on the matter are since the ignorant are such a large part of the population, and since they contribute little more than labor to society, they would be the most expendable. My opinion has not changed. As resources become finite, this is especially important to consider. As automation becomes more pervasive throughout the world, there will be less and less need for so many people.

I know there will be opposition to this. I think the most opposition will come from two sources who often team up to damage society; The Owners and the religious. Think about it. The Owners depend on an ever-increasing mass of people to market their products towards. Furthermore, they need a considerable workforce they can underpay to do the jobs automation is not yet prepared to handle. The religious have their agenda. Following the dictates of their cults, they want to create more followers. They wish to have this multitude, so they outvote the intelligent, as they do so often. The more cult members, the more influence they will have. Also, if they do ever decide to take the country by force, they will have a vast army they can call to fight for them.

Remember, since they have little else to do but work and watch TV, the unintelligent will breed. Well, they will have sex. Breeding will come because too many of them will not be smart enough to use birth control. Given the resistance to birth control and abortion by the various cults, we will be flooded with an excess of human beings in no time.

The stupid cost us money: Perhaps you have heard the expression "If you think education costs a lot, try ignorance." This statement is so true. Ignorance leads to poverty, and poverty leads to crime. Crime is costly. Insurance companies pay out millions each year to recompense victims of crimes. Crime costs everyone. The victims, the insurance companies. If the culprit is captured and sent to prison, it requires the public to house and feed prisoners. The average prisoners are not well educated.

It is not only crime where stupidity costs us money. Many industries have difficulty finding skilled workers. These are still jobs (for now, at least) in manufacturing, construction, and the like. Good paying jobs that go unfilled because people don't want to learn the skills anymore. Why not? It's not like these folks are going to become CEOs of major corporations. Mike Rowe, the former host of the TV show *Dirty Jobs*, has been encouraging young people to learn building trades with an organization called Generation Next. This course is something people could do to gain good-paying jobs. However, most won't. They will say it is too hard. They cannot be bothered. Can this country survive with an unskilled, dim-witted populace? I think not.

The stupid is an embarrassment to us all: As I stated earlier, human history is the story of achievement. The stupid achieve nothing. The United States, once one of the top countries in the world, is progressively failing more and more.

In 2015, the results of the cross-national test known as the Progamme for International Student Assessment (PISA) was released. The assessment is conducted every three years among 15-year-olds. The US placed 38th in math and 24th in science. This poor showing is unacceptable. This lackluster performance is especially true for a country that depends so much on math and science for its defense, economics, and standing in the world.

We cannot blame this all on Trump or even Betsy DeVos, also though I'm sure their horrible influence will soon become apparent. No, there is a deeper problem here—the disrespect and mistrust of education itself. Promoted by the religious, which includes Betsy DeVos, who sees education as elitist and dangerous to their cults, the devaluation of education has been going on for decades now.

In the 1950s, the Russians launched Sputnik. This news sent Americans into a panic. New emphasis was placed on education, particularly math and science. People became excited about the possibilities of space. What did we do with this modern education? We soon overtook the Russians who, to this day, still have never sent a human beyond Earth orbit. We landed on the moon. Humans from the United States walked on the moon, conducted research, and brought back samples. I remember watching Neil Armstrong at something like 2:00 in the morning when he stepped on (more like jumped down to) the lunar surface. Though I was just a kid, I felt great pride in my country. Other missions followed. After that great burst of exploration and achievement, we have not been back to the moon since 1972. That is almost fifty years ago! We should have had a base there by now.

As I said, the religious cults despise education and promote ignorance. This fact is especially true in the southern part of the United States. I lived there for eleven years. I know. This one kid (well, he was about twenty) told me he was stupid and proud of it. He didn't want to be smart like a Yankee. I guess you must have some goals. The irony for me is the most intelligent people I know live down south. I've tried to get them to move up here, but the Atlanta area is their home.

Still, these attitudes are dangerous. Stupid people embarrass our country. Our standing as a leader in education has gone down, and as a leader, in general, has gone down. We must eliminate this virus now before it kills our nation.

The stupid are extremely dangerous: Whenever a society is overrun by people who cannot make intelligent decisions, that country is in danger of collapse. These are people who reject empirical evidence or even know what it is. They prefer alternative facts to real facts. They allow themselves to be ruled by emotion instead of common sense. Too much of the American populace is anti-intellectual. If people celebrate stupidity, as ours does, the nation will fall. Perhaps Thomas Jefferson said it best: "If a nation expects to be ignorant and free, in a state of civilization, it expects what never was and never will be."

BONUS REASON!!! The stupid now have their own president, Donald Trump: Indeed, Trump is the embodiment of all the reasons to kill the stupid cited in this chapter. He is the entire thing in microcosm.

Trump holds us back as a country. Trump didn't do this by himself. However, he is now the figurehead of a backward-looking party that emphasizes greed and power over generosity and caring.

Trump is probably going to start a war. This war will happen because he is incompetent, slightly because he values potential kickbacks from war-profiteers more than American lives.

Trump is easily manipulated. From what we have seen, Trump follows the advice from whoever may have talked to him last. He makes policy decisions based on what he hears on Fox News, treating them like unofficial policy advisors. This trait is strange because Trump likes to manipulate people himself, like his followers. But then, you can't expect consistency from a moron.

Trump is not a good citizen. He puts his interests before the country's interests. This is not a good trait for a president. I doubt he has even read the Constitution. Also though I had problems with other presidents, I never questioned they were doing what they thought best for the country.

Trump believes in at least one fairy tale. I don't think Trump believes in God. That's just a lie he uses to manipulate the religious. I think Trump believes the fairy tale he *is* God. By everything he has said, it is quite apparent he thinks he is the most magnificent human being that has ever lived or will ever live.

Trump denies science and facts. Last year, Trump pulled the United States out of the climate change agreement. This story is science; some 97% of scientists agree on it. He claimed it was a hoax by the Chinese. He has made cuts to scientific agencies such as NASA and the Environmental Protection Agency while putting cronies like Scott Pruitt (now gone) in charge of such agencies. Trump has no understanding or respect for science.

Trump breeds like a rabbit. Well, sort of. At least he can afford his kids. He has children from multiple mothers. Given his record of faithlessness, there may be others. Let's face it; none of these kids are rocket scientists.

Trump costs us money. Are you tired of winning yet? Between his tax cuts for the wealthy and his proposed tariffs, Trump costs Americans vast sums of money. Foreign travelers are leery of coming to the United States, costing us revenue. His desire to build a wall will waste taxpayer money if approved.

Trump is an embarrassment to us all. Acting like a narcissistic idiot in front of world leaders, having no grasp of American history or American law, acting like a cranky three-year-old, undermining trust in American institutions, violating the Emoluments Clause, childishly attempting to erase the legacy of President Barack Obama, being corrupt and allowing corruption. The list goes on and on.

Yes, Donald Trump is the total package. A package of incompetence and corruption. A thieving man-baby who should be living in prison instead of the White House. It was the stupid that put him there. It's our job to take him out.

As you can see, the stupid are very dangerous to our country on many levels. We have now made the ultimate mistake; we have allowed the stupid to become the ruling class in the United States of America. I'm not sure we can still fix this unless we exterminate the stupid from our country. We must no longer be concerned about political correctness. Now we just need to be correct.

It's Getting Hot in Here

Climate change is a fact. Plain and simple. I was skeptical about it at first. That is the proper approach to anything, of course. That is the point when you should learn. I read from different sources. Some that agreed climate change was real and others that said it was not real, even a hoax. The current moron in chief has said it was a hoax perpetrated by the Chinese. I found the information from those who thought climate change to be a severe problem to be the most credible.

Now I should admit I am no expert. I have no degree in climate science, no fieldwork, not even a thermometer hanging by my window. I do, however, have access to books, media, and the Internet. These things give me access to people who do have degrees, fieldwork, and thermometers. If you even do the most casual research, you will find climate change is real, and the evidence is overwhelming. Something like 97-98% of all scientists agrees climate change is a fact. The other 2-3%, the deniers, are either paid shrills or flat out idiots. Think not? Remember, there are still imbeciles who think the Earth is flat.

It is true Earth does go through natural warming and cooling cycles. However, according to the Environmental Protection Agency, the warming we have experienced for the last fifty years cannot be explained by natural phenomena such as changes in the sun or volcanic activity. Oceans are becoming more acidic, and their temperatures are increasing, ice caps are melting, and sea levels are rising.

If you are reading this, I can assume you are already familiar with most of this information. If you are not, or simply wish to learn more, the EPA has an excellent FAQ page. It is on their website: www.epa.gov. NASA also is a great source. Their website is climate.nasa.gov. Hopefully, Trump doesn't have this information removed, as has been implied.

So, what is the cause of climate change? As I'm sure you already know, it's us. Yep, we did it! No denying it! A dog is smart enough to know it shouldn't defecate where it eats, but we don't! Climate scientists will tell you it is the human activity that has brought these changes to the Earth's eco-system. In just about 150 years, we have managed to drive carbon dioxide levels to the moon!

There are things we can do to stop or at least slow down climate change. Switch to electric cars, for instance. They are ideal for city and small town driving. It will be a few more years before they become practical for long-distance excursions, but you could always rent a traditional car for those times you need to drive far. In the meantime, the government could offer tax breaks and incentives to help you buy one. That is if the Owners don't prevent it.

We could establish a carbon tax, as some have suggested. The carbon tax would tax companies based on how much carbon per metric ton they release into the atmosphere.

We can push for the Paris Agreement negotiated in 2016 to be fully restored (President Trump pulled us out of it in 2017, although many states took it upon themselves to rejoin it) implemented and enforced. It was one of the triumphs of Barack Obama's presidency. The agreement should scientifically reduce greenhouse gasses and make the climate more resilient.

Yet another avenue is completely switching power generation to solar and wind. These resources are proving more and more successful around the world. There is even a plan to possibly convert all roads and other tarmac surfaces into energy-generating platforms by covering them with solar panels that are tough enough to be driven upon. These could easily power the entire country if the bugs are worked out. If we ignore the Owners and employ these exciting new technologies, we could save the planet practically overnight.

The best thing we can do is reduce the population rapidly. Without so many people, the production of excess carbon dioxide will also go down immediately. Too many people, or perhaps any other population be it dogs, cats, cows, insects, or whatever, is too damaging to the planet. Add to that a species that can knowingly affect the planet's eco-system but does not make wise decisions, and you have a recipe for disaster. In a previous chapter, I outlined how reducing the population can be achieved. Now we need to do it.

The Dirtiest Game of Them All

Since the dawn of civilization, when humans transformed themselves from hunter/gatherers into societies ruled by emperors and kings, there have been politics. Per Merriam-Webster, one definition of politics is "the art and science of government." Sounds nice, doesn't it? A dignified and moral process used to guide the citizenry for the good of all. The word comes from the Greek: *politikos,* which means "of, for, or relating to citizens." I think most of us would prefer the definition provided by the late Robin Williams: "Politics: "Poli" a Latin word meaning "many"; and "tics" meaning "bloodsucking creatures."

Politics has always been a dirty game. From the time Julius Caesar was assassinated in the Roman Senate to the recent debacle in the United States, where two narcissistic, power-hungry rich people competed to be president, people will do anything to gain and keep power. That is the real purpose of politics, to fool the gullible. Abraham Lincoln, one of the few noble politicians, famously said: "You can fool all the people some of the time, and some of the people all the time, but you cannot fool all the people all the time." That may no longer be the case. Through the use of social media, paid for "journalists," fake news stories, and other means, it turns out you CAN fool all the people all the time. Or at least something close to it.

Our once sacred news outlets, bastions of truth in our world, can no longer be trusted. The Owners own them. Giant conglomerates control the news to push their narrative onto the world and, therefore, their candidates. Time-Warner owns CNN; NBC is owned by Comcast, Fox by Rupert Murdoch, and so on. Through these communication empires, the Owners control public opinion.

Furthermore, using their puppets in the government, they are seeking to destroy independent news companies that won't kowtow to them. They are doing this under the guise of fighting fake news outlets. I provide the solution to that in another chapter.

It doesn't stop there. Campaigns lie, cheat, steal, do whatever they can to get an advantage over their opponents. It has always been that way. If you're an older reader, you remember the Watergate scandal. On June 17th, 1972, five men were caught breaking into the Democratic Party's national headquarters. It was to be eventually discovered the burglars (referred to as "plumbers") were working for the Committee to Re-elect the President.

Interestingly, the acronym for that was CREEP. They were part of President Richard Nixon's "dirty tricks" campaign, used against anyone Nixon hated, feared or mistrusted. Nixon was very paranoid. He kept a list of enemies. Although Nixon did not give the order for the break-in (that was John Mitchell, his former Attorney General and head of CREEP), he participated in the cover-up. The strange thing is it was all so unnecessary. Nixon went on to win in a landslide over George McGovern, the incredibly weak Democratic candidate. Eventually, this leads to Nixon being forced to resign. Ultimately, Nixon was pardoned by succeeding President Gerald Ford. If you are rich and/or powerful, you can get away with anything. A great message to send the American people. Still, Nixon did accomplish some good things. He ended the Vietnam War, opened China to the West, and established the Environmental Protection Agency. Nixon did become something of an "elder statesman" before he died. However, the Watergate scandal forever scarred his presidency.

I'm sure everyone has received calls and robocalls from campaigns. Some of you have gotten e-mails as well. This story is a personal anecdote, I know it is true, but you don't, having no proof to show you beyond the e-mails themselves. So, take it for what it is worth. Here is an e-mail I got, supposedly from a former girlfriend, back in October 2016. One month before the election:

"So here we are in October ...weeks away from an election that will make or BREAK America !! It will become the hunger games ..and Katniss I'm not! I do hope you are listening to Bernie and will put your vote out for Hillary!!! How is it going?? Still here in Jersey loving all that Christie can do for you!!! I thought about you the other day when I saw an endless shrimp commercial .... Maybe we could meet up for lunch or dinner sometime...... Take care, XXXX."

I dated this woman for five or six years. Not once did we ever discuss politics. I suspect it was a shill for Hillary Clinton, probably paid to hack into people's e-mail accounts and impersonate them to persuade others to vote for her. I fell for the first e-mail, but then I got suspicious. The reference to the character from *The Hunger Games* started me thinking the writer was younger, and the pro-Hillary stance suggested something sneaky was going on. The other idiot (Trump) was at least being open. That is unless all that stuff about Russia influencing the election for him is real.

The point is politics and politicians are not to be trusted. They will say anything and do anything to get elected and go back on their promises as soon as they get into office. As Donald Trump supporters are now realizing, he outright lied to them. He will not save American jobs despite the phony show he made of it with Carrier. He will not end Obamacare; he will not build a wall. He won't even try to put Hillary Clinton in prison, the one thing I wanted him to do. Trump also promised to "drain the swamp" of special interests in Washington. What did he do? Trump filled it with even more toxic waste than was there before. He filled his cabinet with billionaires and ex-military whackos. The goal is the official corporate takeover of the United States. Welcome to The Corporate States of America.

It is interesting to note some of our Founding Fathers were opposed to political parties. James Madison and Alexander Hamilton wrote about this danger of political parties in No. 9 and No. 10 of the Federalist Papers. George Washington was never a member of a party. In his farewell address of 1796, he expressed they should not be formed. They knew partisanship could tear the country apart. They were right. Furthermore, political parties invariably fall victim to greed and corruption, as we have recently seen.

You already know this, of course. The question is, how do we clean a pool that has been mucked up for millennia, long before our country was even founded? It is a global problem. We need a comprehensive solution. Let's concentrate on this country first since it the largest country that has fallen victim to the Owners. If we can straighten this country out, maybe we can fix this world after all. The road is going to be long and hard. It will no doubt take longer than our lifetimes, but we have to start somewhere. We can begin by impeaching this president and his entire administration. Throw them all out and hold a new special election with honest candidates. The difficulty I see is there is no provision in the Constitution for special elections. The Founders never realized we would screw ourselves up so badly.

We can continue this with strict regulations for politicians and other officials. Lobbying should be made illegal. Anti-corruption acts should be passed in every state and eventually at the federal level. No one occupying public office is to have any ties to anything outside of that office. Any business is to be sold, any dubious relationships (business, church, friend or family member) are to be broken off for both the candidate and any immediate family member. The official must supply weekly reports as to their activities. They will be monitored by an agency of citizens set up for the task with at least one other agency tracking them as well.

If an official does get past the safeguards for a time but then is caught, the punishment must be severe. After conviction, I suggest he/she be put to death. The government confiscates their property with no consideration for their families. Their remains ground into animal feed or powder, so nothing remains of their existence. Okay, so it's a bit much. Of course, those who are inclined to be corrupt naturally assume they will be able to weasel their way out of this. However, I think after the first few executions, they will fall in line.

As to the central agency responsible for monitoring the officials, it depends. I see this agency assigning one monitor to watch just one or two officials. If the official were smart enough to fool the monitor legitimately, the only punishment would be a pay reduction, either temporary or semi-permanent, which he/she could eventually work up from. However, if the monitor was taking bribes or otherwise in cahoots with the official, the monitor will suffer the same fate as the official—the corrupt steal from all of us. I have no patience with evil. Neither should you.

President Trump offers us the perfect opportunity to start putting these reforms into practice. As the most corrupt president ever, he is destroying our status in the world. He does not know or even care what he is doing. Trump has only been in office for a short time yet is already under investigation for multiple crimes. There is a movement to impeach him that grows every day. It will happen unless Republicans repeat history and march over to the White House to tell Trump, as they did with Richard Nixon, that his support in Congress has collapsed. The intention is to force him to resign.

This resignation cannot happen. I do not think it will happen anyway. The Republican march to the White House may happen, but Trump won't resign. He is too madly egotistical to do that. To him, quitting would be a sign of weakness. In his mind, this is his country. He won it. He owns it. He is not going to give it up. This might be the point when Trump goes full-on dictator.

There are other reasons Trump should not be forced to resign, even if it were possible. Trump must be punished. He must leave office in disgrace. Furthermore, Trump must be executed for his crimes. This process will be messy, of course. It will be the first time an American president will go not only through full impeachment but the execution. The political impulse always just does what must be done, get it over with and move on. We cannot do that this time. There are reasons for this. First, there is a need for what I call societal revenge. Trump has hurt all of us. He needs to suffer as we have suffered. He needs to lose everything: his fortune, his liberty, and his life. The more important reason is the world must see this happen. We must send out the clear message that corruption like this will not be tolerated, and those that commit it will be punished. What do you think would have been done with Adolph Hitler if he had been captured alive? He would have been tried and then executed. Trump deserves no less.

Get Rid of Them All

There has been a lot of talk concerning getting rid of President Donald Trump. Many people, including those who voted for him, realize he has got to go. This path is easier said than done. Congress must impeach the president. That is not likely to happen to a Republican president while Republicans control both the House and Senate. Even though many Republicans hate him too, he is the useful idiot they need to push their agenda. Once Republicans get what they want to benefit the Owners and themselves, then they might consider impeaching Trump. This way, they can blame everything on him even if he didn't do it. People can scream all they want, but Trump is not going to go until Republicans and their Owners decide they want to get rid of him.

You may have heard that Trump is angering the "Deep State." The supposed deep state is defined as the "state within the state" or shadow government that is really in charge of the United States. According to this fable, the military and the intelligence agencies are our true masters. They ultimately decide if they will be loyal to the president or will throw him out, possibly by assassination. This story is very like the idea the world is run by a secret cabal of the rich headed by the Rothschild family. For the most part, these are conspiracy theories. However, in the United States, the rich do indeed run this country. It is not an organized movement per se; it is just the way business is done in America. The rich all go to the same places, restaurants, clubs, vacation spots, and so on. What do you think they talk about when they get together? They figured out a long time ago the way you run a country is by buying up all the politicians. Owners don't like Trump, whom they see as too unpredictable because he does not need to be for sale.

That may change. The stock market topped 21,000 for the first time. If this continues, the Owners will warm to Trump. Trump is eliminating the regulations huge corporations hate. These actions will increase their profits. They like that. So even though the Owners are wary of Trump, they and their bought and paid for politicians (they own the Democrats too, by the way) will be more than happy to tolerate Trump, at least until he screws things up so bad they will have to act.

What if they do act and impeach Donald Trump? Then we will get Mike Pence, a religious fanatic who is no more qualified than Trump, albeit in different ways. What will we be gaining? Even if you could pressure Congress to impeach Pence too, you will get the Speaker of the House as president. Currently, but not for much longer,

Paul Ryan. You will also still have 435 members in the House of Representatives and 100 members of the Senate to deal with. All of them, except for three or four, do not have your best interests at heart. We can't impeach them all. Or can we?

Nope. Just like only Congress can impeach the president and vice-president, only the House can impeach House members, and only the Senate can impeach senators. That is in Article I and II of the Constitution. Unfortunately, life is not like classic fantasy literature where you can destroy the head of the evil, and all the attendant darkness falls away. We could petition Congress to amend the Constitution to allow the people to impeach directly, but what of the odds of them doing that? We would still need to replace almost the entire Congress. Not being a lawyer, I'm not sure how that can be done. Any ideas? If we could do it, we could impeach them all, hold hearings to see who has helped the people and who has helped themselves. Those politicians who have supported the people should return to the office so they can continue their excellent work. The others will be executed publicly. I would like to see it done on the National Mall by the guillotine. Those who passed the hearing and the new members of Congress will know they have the sword of Damocles over their heads. This effect will ensure they will work for the people, not the

Owners. Maybe we should just march into the Capital building and do it. I do not want to overthrow the government, only the people in government. They have backstabbed us and continue to do so.

There was a radio host named Jim Gearhart, who advocated for what he called GRIP, Get Rid of Incumbent Politicians. He suggested the only way to clean things up is to keep voting everyone out until they get the message and fly right. That seems to be a sound strategy to start, but I would add, save those who have done an excellent job but get the rest out. So this means you must learn who these people are at every level. I admit I have not done such an excellent job of that myself, particularly at the local levels, but I need to learn. So do you.

So, while I would instead march into the Capital, put them on trial, then drag them out for beheading, we may need to take another approach if we want to avoid a civil war, which may come anyway if the Trumpies and religionists get their way. Let's try to do what we must do more or less the traditional way. Get intelligent and honest Atheist and Humanist candidates to run for office. Create tests to make sure potential candidates understand United States history and government with an emphasis on the Constitution. Require all officials to take their oath of office on the Constitution if elected. Once installed in office, they can either call for the popular impeachment as I described above or push to impeach disreputable politicos themselves. This solution will be hard at first, but if we can get enough honest people in office, perhaps we can get impeachments like I described to come to pass. At this point, we could follow the recommendations I made in another chapter for regulating politicians. Eventually, bringing them to the state legislatures and the governorships as well. While there are already procedures in place to deal with this sort of thing, they are rarely followed. One way or another, popular impeachment *must* come to pass. The future of this country depends on it.

Hated He Won, Glad She Lost

We are now in the presidency of Donald Trump. Without any doubt, Trump is the least qualified but most narcissistic idiot ever to hold the office. Everyone knows this, Democrats, Republicans, and almost everyone breathing except for the stupid and proud of it crowd, which got him elected. The rest of the world is looking at us as if we are, as Rocky Balboa would put it, mentally irregular. Who can blame them? Trump has advocated for policies that are arguably insane. He has installed a cabinet that seems dedicated to dismantling the departments they are to lead. He continues to go on about his victory in November and the size of the crowd at his inauguration despite the reports of the agencies who track this sort of thing and photographic evidence.

So, the question remains. How did this bombastic, thin-skinned moron become President of the United States? The answer lies, in part, to the dissolving of both main political parties. Both parties have become corrupt and unresponsive to their bases. Voters think their parties have abandoned them, and they are right. Neither party cares about you. Republicans, while always pro-business (Owners), gradually became more corrupt over the years. This trend was particularly showcased in the presidency of Richard "I am not a crook" Nixon. The Democrats made their Faustian deal in the 1990s, courtesy of President Bill "Slick Willie" Clinton. When Clinton almost single-handedly, with the possible help but definitely the approval of wife and "former" Goldwater Girl Hillary Clinton, established the corporatist wing of the Democratic Party. That wing took over, and the progressives of Franklin Delano Roosevelt retreated to the fringe.

Let's look at Donald Trump first. Trump beat out the biggest field of Republican losers ever put out to run for president. The group included Carly Fiorina, who ran Hewitt-Packard into the ground and Dr. Ben Carson, a brilliant surgeon but total lunatic. Trump steamrolled over all of them. He did it because he was an experienced television personality who knows how to play to the crowd. Trump sold the perception he was a robust and decisive person who already had all the country's problems solved in his head. He just needed to get into the office so he could do them. People like that. I think most people want to be told what to do and what to think. They want simple solutions to complex problems. People like this cannot understand subtle nuances either because of willing ignorance or poor education. We all remember how much Trump loves "the poorly educated," as he said on February 24, 2016. Add alt-right morons, racist idiots, and treasonous religionists, and you have a toxic recipe for the downfall of the United States.

Believe it or not, some Trump supporters are not mindless nincompoops. There was a significant proportion who voted for Trump not because they saw him as some kind of savior but because they saw him as somebody different. They wanted to shake things up, and they did. These were people who felt disenfranchised and ignored by both parties. No one was listening to them.

Interestingly enough, many of them would have voted for Bernie Sanders before the nomination was stolen from him. More about that later. Trump was smart enough to pay them lip service, which Hillary Clinton did not.

To all these people, Trump was the strongman leader they were looking for. His racism, misogyny, narcissism, contempt for the poor, greed, ignorance, immaturity, insensitivity, and overall scumbagginess did not matter. All they saw was a white knight who would let them indulge in their dual delusion that they were somehow being picked on, and they should be on top. This way of thinking is what having a stupid electorate leads to. Of course, the Republicans do not have that market cornered.

The Democrats have a wide swath of stupid in their party as well. Democrats are as greedy and moronic as their Republican counterparts. They proved this to the entire world during the 2016 campaign. The one-time party of the people had become the party of corporatist lackeys thanks to Bill Clinton, who sold the party out in the 1990s. Since Bill Clinton had already served the Constitutionally mandated two terms as president, he passed the baton to his equally greedy, even more narcissistic wife, Hillary. Now, this is just a feeling I have had, but it seemed Hillary Clinton possessed a sense of entitlement to the presidency. Others I talked to agree with me. What do you think?

It does not matter. Let's focus on Hillary herself. I am not going to dwell on Benghazi, her peddling of influence at the State Department, the Clinton Foundation, or any of the other Clinton scandals. Some of them may be made up nonsense by Republicans; others may be real. I want to focus only on the things we know for a fact she has said or done. With that said, time to move on. On the pro side, Hillary Clinton is a highly experienced politician. She served as both a senator and Secretary of State in addition to being First Lady. Clinton knows how to conduct herself on both the national and international stages. She probably knows all the movers and shakers of the world. On the surface, Hillary Clinton would have made an excellent president. Unfortunately, Hillary

Clinton's cons far outnumber her pros. She is known for being a warmonger, as noted in a New York Times Magazine article from April 21, 2016. She seems to prefer interventionist wars for profit. Hillary is also a fan of regime change but not considering the consequences of those changes. She is known to be a liar, like Donald Trump. Case in point, her famous landing in Bosnia under sniper fire, which was later revealed by news footage to be a very peaceful landing on the tarmac. She claimed she "misremembered." How do you misremember if someone shot at you or not? Her notorious flip-flopping on gay marriage. Before 2013, she was against it. It was her husband who signed the Defense of Marriage Act as well as Don't Ask, Don't Tell. Now, after the country became more gay-friendly, Hillary was suddenly for gay marriage. Add to that her secretiveness, her "public" and "private" positions, promotion of fracking, her silence on the Dakoda Access Pipeline, and her advocacy for Wall Street and the attendant fees for speaking to them. Hillary was already damaged goods, considered untrustworthy by a large number (most?) of the public. As such, Hillary Clinton was a terrible candidate for the Democrats, who still tried to claim they were the party of the people.

All this would seem like polling booth poison, but strangely enough, the Democrats decided to go with Hillary. There was an equally qualified candidate who ran against her, who was far more accessible, who had no scandals connected with his name. Of course, this was Senator Bernie Sanders of Vermont. The people loved him. They still do. He always polled at least ten points ahead of Trump while Clinton struggled to stay one or two points ahead, sometimes falling behind. The problem was, the Democratic National Committee (DNC) wanted that big corporate money that Sanders had refused, preferring to raise his campaign money from the people themselves. Hillary started with a war chest of 128 million (as opposed to Donald Trump's 94 million) but burned (Berned?) through most of it just fighting Sanders. She needed to raise more money towards the end, as at her famous Denver fund-raiser, where she used a white noise machine, so the press could not hear what she was telling the big donors.

Throughout the primaries, Hillary, along with her toady Debbie Wasserman Shultz who was the DNC chair at the time, schemed to get Sanders out of the race. They accomplished this by voter suppression, particularly in Arizona and Brooklyn, NY, as well as other nefarious acts, to steal the primaries for Hillary. The DNC "put its finger on the primaries" as it was put. Wasserman Shultz does not go to the bathroom without clearing it with Hillary first. At the Democratic National Convention, this was found out, and Shultz was booed off the stage and either quit or was fired shortly thereafter. Of course, Clinton was right there with a new job for her loyal weasel. The new temporary chair, Donna Brazile, found herself in hot water when it was discovered she had given the questions to the CNN held presidential debate (Brazile was a contributor to CNN at the time) to Hillary's campaign. Also, at the convention, they blocked many Sanders' supporters from coming in and hired seat fillers for the empty seats. Brazile would later write a book where she revealed Clinton mainly bought the DNC by resolving their financial debt allowing "in exchange for raising money and investing in the DNC, Hillary would control the party's finances, strategy, and all the money raised." – *Hacks: The Inside Story of the Break-ins and Breakdowns That Put Donald Trump in the White House* by Donna Brazille.

Despite all this, which I consider an act of treason, Hillary Clinton was now the Democratic nominee. Now perceived as being even more untrustworthy by the electorate, she hit the trail for the general election. Clinton had the backing of most of the corporate-owned media like CNN (who always underreported on Bernie Sanders but overreported on Trump and Clinton) as well as the money-hungry DNC. Some say Clinton lost because she took the month of August off the campaign trail to raise money to make up funds she spent staving off Sanders, others say it was because she did not campaign in vital swing states like Wisconsin. I agree this is true, but I think the main reason she lost, besides her untrustworthiness and passing relationship with the truth, is she ignored rural people. This reason is not totally her fault. It is a strategy the Democrats have used for years.

Democrats concentrate on densely populated areas. It makes sense to them because that is where they assume most of their base will be. This action was a mistake, which they are now realizing. Democrats ignore these people, "the deplorables" as Clinton put them. Trump, at least, acknowledged their existence. Yes, most of them were poor and/or stupid, but with Trump, they were not ignored. The people wanted something different, and the Democrats didn't give it to them. The only Democrat that did not ignore these people was, you guessed it, Bernie Sanders. If the DNC were not so greedy and shortsighted, Sanders would have gotten those votes and be president today.

As you see, I blame the Democrats and Hillary Clinton for Trump's win. The DNC even admitted it in open court, in response to a lawsuit by Sanders supporters including myself, they had the right to pick anyone they wanted to be the candidate. They made a claim they are a private corporation and, therefore, need not be responsive to the people who support them. So, their acts cannot be treasonous, can they? One would think the beaten Democrats would learn their lesson. They haven't. The DNC might rerun Hillary Clinton in 2020. I guess they figure the third time might be the charm. If she doesn't run, they might go with Cory Booker (another Democratic corporatist) or perhaps Oprah Winfrey (great, another TV idiot) to show how "progressive" they are. Sanders has also expressed interest in 2020. By that point, he will be 79 or 80 years old. Still, Bernie strikes me that as being pretty spry. Perhaps he could run with Tulsi Gabbard? In any case, he needs to run as an independent. As for Hillary, she (and daughter Chelsea who is also threatening a run for office) needs to go away. It will be hard enough to get lunatic Trump, who will now be entrenched if not previously impeached, out of the office. We don't need to battle another criminal as well.

Was Trump Sent by God?

God is sitting on his throne in Heaven when George W. Bush comes up.
God asks Bush, "What do you believe?"
Bush answers, "I believe in freedom and opportunity."
God says, "Very good. Come sit at my right."
Following Bush is Barack Obama.
God asks Obama, "What do you believe?"
Obama answers, "I believe in peace and love."
God says, "Very good. Come sit at my left."
The next to approach God's throne is Donald Trump.
God asks Trump, "What do you believe?"
Trump answers, "I believe you are sitting in my chair."

It was a joke a friend sent to me awhile back. It's funny and utterly consistent with Donald Trump's ego. I don't think Trump believes in the Abrahamic god any more than I do. I think the only god he believes in is the one he sees in the mirror every morning. It is not surprising. It has been known for decades Donald Trump is a narcissistic, misogynistic fool. He is greedy, bigoted, dishonest, and unethical. Trump always lies and is most likely paranoid and delusional. He is proud of being a philanderer, cheating on wives with playmates and porn stars. Trump is the kind of guy you wouldn't buy a used car from. Somehow, Donald Trump became President of the United States.

In the ordinary political world, Trump would be polling booth poison. His shunning of "family values" should have doomed him from the start. In our current bizarre world, this is not the case. His immoral behavior is what his followers admire about him! Trump's most ardent support comes from evangelical Christians. You know, the folks who *preach* against these things! In the strange world of the religious right, these once negative traits are now seen as positives.

As a Humanist, I find this particularly amusing. Much Christian literature rails against Humanist situational ethics. It is true. Humanists think the case itself often defines the ethics of a situation. God-worshippers think ethics (what they call "morality") are unchanging because their god-thing has dictated them. In the age of Trump, their morality has become much more flexible.

Let's look at some of Trump's positions and policies. Like most Republicans, President Trump is against anything that helps people despite what he says. In 2016 he said he would solve the California drought. He did that by simply declaring, "There is no drought." Trump does not accept climate change despite scientific evidence, so he pulled the United States out of the Paris climate agreement. He got a tax break for everyone but neglected to mention that break would end in ten years for the average person but would go on forever for the rich. Trump rolled back EPA protections against polluters and FDA protections on food safety (this last one is odd since, according to Michael Wolff's book, *Fire and Fury*, Trump fears being poisoned.) He has consistently cut any regulations that interfere with him lining his pockets. He has repeatedly sabotaged the Affordable Care Act (Obamacare) because he could not get rid of it. He wants to keep out refugees and immigrants, not just illegal immigrants, all immigrants. Most famously, he wants to build a wall on the Mexican border (which I think is just another attempt to bilk the taxpayers.) Everything Trump does is an action against people.

Now you would think church folks would be against that sort of thing. No doubt some of them are. But look at how many of them support Trump. The most important part of his base is evangelical Christians. Evangelical leaders say things like, "If you are against Trump, you are against God!" Considering their leaders are con artists like Robert Jeffries, Paula White, Jim Bakker, Tony Perkins, and Franklin Graham, it makes me happy I'm an Atheist. I recall seeing a drawing on Facebook of Jesus hugging Donald Trump in the Oval Office. It plays well into the Christian fantasy of Trump and themselves. Trump is their Christian White Knight. The hero who will vanquish foreigners, globalists, liberals, and political correctness from the land. It also feeds their delusion the United States is a Christian nation as embodied by Joe McNaughton in his infamous painting *One Nation Under God,* which depicts Jesus, having just written the Constitution, presenting it to the American people. Behind him are the Founding Fathers and well as other notables such as Abraham Lincoln. In front are good people (on his right, of course) and bad secular people on his left. If you would like one, it is available on McNaughton's website and at better truck-stops everywhere.

The Bible is an amazingly versatile book. You can always find a Bible passage that supports practically any position you wish to take, even if they conflict with each other. For instance, look at these two passages concerning burdens. In Galatians 6:2, we are told: "Bear one another's burdens, and so fulfill the law of Christ." Just three verses later, Galatians 6:5, we are advised: "Each man will have to bear his own load." Genesis 2:17: Adam was told that if and when he eats the forbidden fruit, he would die the same day. Genesis 5:5: Adam ate the fruit and went on to live to a ripe old age of 930 years. These examples came from a site called *answering-Christianity*. I did double-check them with my own KJV Bible. Now it is to be expected there would be differences in the Biblical accounts as in the telling of any story, mainly mythological stories. The problem is people base their lives on these tales. They are not even consistent, and preachers use these passages to shore up whatever they want their followers to believe.

It seems inconceivable how anyone who claims they love and care about people could support a lying, bloviating, dishonest fool totally in love with himself like Donald Trump. After the protests in Charlottesville, where a young woman was killed, Trump said there were good people "on both sides." Really? One of those sides were white supremacist Nazis! Trump does not even have the decency to condemn the Nazis. Still, religious types support him. It is quite telling. It demonstrates god-worshippers will prop up any lunatic who will give them what they want, no matter who gets hurt. It also goes to show how bankrupt the entire idea of morality is. I have no morals myself. Morals are arbitrary rules created by old men to rule the sex lives of human beings, particularly women. I have ethics, which tell you what's right. Those who support Donald Trump are hypocrites. Hypocrisy, thy name is Christian.

Conservative Whackos and Liberal Idiots

This writing is another essay I have been hesitant to write. I think after it is read, I will lose whatever friends I still have. Human beings tend to group themselves. Sometimes, we arrange ourselves in ways that are harmless such as our interests, the sports we like, the books we read, the movies we go to, and the like. Other times we group ourselves by ethnic background, religion, economic status, intelligence levels, and so forth. It is tribalism in action.

As we have seen, some forms of tribalism are quite dangerous. We see this in religion every day. The religions, which are organized into various cults that present different levels of danger to society. These range from being reasonably benign to outright militant.

Although religion will play into it, as Christopher Hitchens pointed out, religion poisons everything; this essay, however, is focused on politics, mainly how we have grouped ourselves into two camps; conservative and liberal. You notice I didn't mention moderates. For the most part, I'm not so sure they exist anymore. Everyone seems to be one or the other. There is no middle ground anymore. We have two competing worldviews fighting for supremacy, and neither one will give an inch.

For purposes of this argument, only I will use the political party terms "Republican" and "Democrat" interchangeably with "conservative" and "liberal." I do this only as a kind of shorthand since the two parties represent these two viewpoints in most peoples' minds. Truth to tell, not every Republican is so hardline conservative, and not all Democrats are so staunchly liberal. I am only addressing the issues and political parties as they are *now*. Political parties change over time. The Republicans were founded as a progressive party opposed to slavery. Democrats once supported the Ku Klux Klan.

Let's start with conservatives. Here is how Merriam-Webster defines it:

2 a: tending or disposed to maintain existing views, conditions, or institutions:
traditional
- *conservative* policies

b: marked by moderation or caution
- a *conservative* estimate

c: marked by or relating to conventional norms of taste, elegance, style, or manners
- a *conservative* suit
- a *conservative* architectural style

So being conservative, as I understand the term, refers to someone who supports traditional norms and attitudes. They resist change. However, when they are provided with evidence, they *will* change. In other words, once the wisdom of a new paradigm is witnessed, they will accept it and adapt. That's also a good definition of a skeptic. The mantra of skeptics, when confronted by something new, is "Prove it!" To me, that is a true conservative or should be.

Unfortunately, that is not what conservative stands for now. Now the term has been hijacked by Republicans. Republicans and their Owners, the huge corporations and banks, are determined to amass all the wealth of this country for themselves. In their minds, this makes sense, because God determined they should have stewardship over everything. To this end, they are big supporters of the religious cults, who believe in this same hierarchy with the exception that they, the cult leaders, should be on top.

Republicans, like the cults, have a meanness about them. The poor have no value to them. I once heard former Congressman Stephen Fincher (R-TN) say, paraphrasing 2 Thessalonians 3:10: "If you don't work, you shouldn't eat." Can't you feel the love? It is possible I am quoting this out of context, but it is undoubtedly the context Fincher meant. What Fincher doesn't mention is many poor do work, but they still cannot eat, at least as much as they should because they are not paid decent wages. Some companies, such as Walmart and McDonalds, pay so little that workers must get government help to make ends meet even though these huge companies can more than afford to pay them fairly.

This meanness and greed are the recurring themes throughout Republican, religious, and conservative culture. Let us not forget false patriotism, love of militarism, and authoritarianism that is creeping into our country. Why love your neighbor when it is easier to hate them instead? That's the real problem. The people themselves have bought into these false narratives. Republicans are so good at manipulating people, especially our moronic President Trump, that Americans no longer trust their institutions. Most people who are not that bright, to begin with (which is why we need to kill the stupid) accept whatever they are told without questioning. When Republicans do lie, they stick with it, no matter how incorrect or just plain crazy it is. Every day, they prove Joseph Goebbels correct when he said: "If you tell a lie big enough and keep repeating it, people will eventually come to believe it."

As a consequence of this steady diet of falsehoods and hate generated by politicians and preachers, people are becoming more distrustful and less idealistic. Human beings seek security and detest ambivalence. It is why they embrace the hierarchy of God, king, men, women, and children. They like the idea of a "pre-ordained' life and social order. It comforts them. To obtain it, people will even vote against their own best interests.

We will now turn our attention to liberals. Once again, I will still call upon Merriam-Webster for the relevant part of their definition:

5 broad-minded: *especially*: not bound by authoritarianism, orthodoxy, or traditional forms
6 a: of, favoring, or based upon the principles of liberalism
b *capitalized*: of or constituting a political party advocating or associated with the laws of political liberalism

So being liberal is broad-minded. You could also add progressive, willing to explore new ideas that could be beneficial and, at least, how liberals see themselves, more caring.

The Democrats had been the party of Franklin Delano Roosevelt. During Roosevelt's four terms in office, he guided the United States out of the Great Depression and through most of World War II. It was Roosevelt who brought the New Deal and other reforms. He believed in a living wage for everyone, stating: "No business which depends for existence on paying less than living wages to its workers has any right to continue in this country. By living wages, I mean more than a bare subsistence level — I mean the wages of a decent living."

Roosevelt was a good man who defied the privilege of his upper-class upbringing to help the ordinary person truly. The United States became prosperous again and remained so. Even a world war could not slow it down. (Unfortunately, war is also good for the economy) The country didn't face economic problems again until the 1970s.

In the 1960s, liberalism became even more pronounced with the advancement of civil rights, counterculture, anti-war, and (later) gay rights movements. It seemed the pendulum had swung towards a happier, more open future. However, there was pushback. The status quo does not relinquish its position so quickly. Both sides dug in. That struggle is still going on today in what is known as the Culture War.

People tend to change as they grow older and become more conservative. So it is with political parties as well. The Republican Party, which started as the liberal party, eventually became the Grand Old Party of greed, religiosity, and hate. The Democrat Party, once filled with southern white supremacists, became progressive mainly because of Franklin Roosevelt. The white supremacists eventually moved to the Republicans, where they still are today.

The Democrats would soon face another change. The coming of Bill Clinton's "New Democrats." Supposedly, these were Democrats who were fiscally conservative but socially liberal. That didn't last long if it ever did at all. They would evolve into what we now call Corporate Democrats. Corporate Democrats are every bit as money-hungry as Republicans. They are not to be trusted. Hillary Clinton is a Corporate Democrat.

Hillary Clinton brings into focus something I cannot stand about liberals. Very often, they will support something or someone that makes no sense. I think many liberals supported Hillary simply because she is a woman. They were willing to ignore her dishonesty and sneakiness, so they could tout how liberal they are. Clinton is a con artist on the scale of Donald Trump. She spent millions on buying the Democratic Party to ensure she would be the candidate for president. As much as I would like to see a woman president, I could not and would not vote for Clinton simply *because* she is a woman. I wrote in my vote for Bernie Sanders.

In politics, Democrats and Republicans (liberals and conservatives) can easily be spotted by their approach to regulations. Liberals want to regulate everything, while conservatives don't want to regulate anything at all. Currently, there is a proposal to regulate flavors in tobacco products. The rationale is if the tastes are not as pleasant, this will encourage people to quit. It will most likely be supported by Democrats, claiming it makes tobacco safer. It will be opposed by Republicans claiming it is another intrusion on our freedoms. The fact is this is unnecessary. If you are still stupid enough to use tobacco products after over fifty years of warnings by the various health agencies, all the regulation in the world is not going to matter. All it does is make liberals look like idiots and conservatives look like champions of freedom. The net result is no one will take liberals seriously when they try to regulate things that should be regulated, like unethical business practices, environmental issues, and guns. It accounts for why Democrats often lose in middle America. They allow themselves to be perceived as the party that wants to control everything (like Communists!) while Republicans come off as the "do as you want, we won't regulate you" party.

Whether you identify as "liberal" or "conservative," any position you take must be based on reason, logic, and when it is applicable, science. Humans are too tied up in emotion, so they support viewpoints that make no sense. Often this comes from ignorance. It can also come from being lied to by entities that want to control you and/or society. Religionists and politicians are always trying to influence you. Sometimes for good, most of the time not.

Consequently, we talk *at* each other instead of talking *to* each other. Compromise becomes impossible because we are too emotionally invested in our views to see another way. I am probably guilty of this. I like to think of myself as being as dispassionate as they come, but I don't always succeed. I am trying to do better. Maybe all of us need to as well.

Who's Got the Energy?

We need energy. We want it. How do we get it? That's the question that is plaguing society. It's not so much a question of if there is enough energy to power the world. Of course, there is! It is clean and renewable. There is enough to power the entire planet for the next 15 billion years. It involves no digging in the ground for materials that will eventually be exhausted at the cost of clean air and water. The technology already exists to implement use and profitability.

I'm sure you already know I'm talking about solar energy. Throughout the world, solar energy use is becoming more common, even in the United States. However, in this country, there is a sizeable organized opposition to it. It mainly comes from the big oil companies, but opposition comes from some unions and ordinary people as well. It strikes me as strange when you consider if we replace oil with solar energy and other renewable power sources, we could tell those barbaric Middle Eastern countries where they could shove their oil.

The reason oil companies oppose solar energy is evident, greed. Well, greed and an understandable desire to preserve their businesses. They have invested billions of dollars over the past 100 years or so in the various processes to obtain oil. They do not wish to see all that money go to waste. However, it MUST go to waste. Oil is not sustainable. There are only so many decaying dinosaurs in the world. We will not find any oil on the moon either. Oil (and coal) are dead technologies. What these companies need to do now is switch focus to become clean energy companies.

It is where unions and ordinary people come in. Coal and oil have provided good livings for thousands upon thousands of people and their families. Now they see those jobs going away. "...these jobs are going boys and they ain't coming back..." as Bruce Springsteen sang in *"My Hometown."* It does not matter what anyone, a presidential candidate or otherwise, says. Those jobs are gone forever.

There is hope. Yes, jobs will go away, but new posts will come in their stead. People can be re-trained. Along with a much smaller population, we should be able to create steady employment for those who remain.

Solar energy is offering exciting possibilities. Solar can potentially produce more energy than other technologies combined because it works with the limitless (for now) power of the sun. Humans will be long gone from this planet, either because we became extinct or because we left before the sun runs out of energy. We probably won't even need wind power, although we could use it as back up. Solar panels could be put on everyone's roofs. Elon Musk has created a new type of solar roof panel that looks like traditional roof tiles. Another company is developing photovoltaic pavers for use on roadways. They are designed to handle the weight of semi-trucks, are fitted with LEDs to eliminate the need for paint, are pressure sensitive to light up if an obstruction or animal is crossing the road, and even heat up in winter to melt ice and snow. How exciting is that? Our roadway system could become our entire power system as well.

With all this energy coming in, we can easily power the entire Earth with electricity from clean solar power together with wind. We must free ourselves from defunct energy methods of the past and look to a clean and bright future.

Fix the Economy

I was a staunch capitalist my entire life. I always felt capitalism was the best way for economies to run and improve people's lives. In recent years, my opinion has changed dramatically. Capitalism, at least sizeable corporate capitalism, has failed us. It has created the economic inequality everyone talks about. Corporations see themselves as self-governing bodies who owe no allegiance to their countries, its peoples, or even to their employees.

These attitudes had existed at least since the end of the Civil War when the corporate giants of their day, men like Carnegie and Rockefeller, began to demand the government intercede for them in labor and trade disputes. American companies and I imagine companies in other countries as well, had no problem dealing with unscrupulous people and countries, including Nazi Germany if they thought they could get what they wanted from it.

What they want are wealth and power. It seems the ultimate goal is for corporations, whom I still call the Owners in honor of the great George Carlin, is indeed world domination. Political entities, such as nations, only exist to give the average person a sense they have some control over their lives. This last presidential election shows how little control there is. The two leading candidates were an Owner (Trump) and an Owner wannabe (Clinton), both of whom want corporations to rule to some extent. Donald Trump thinks the country should be run as a business (so did Ross Perot, remember him?); therefore, he thinks he just can fire anybody he wants to and make up laws on the fly in violation of the Constitution. Clinton feels pretty much the same way. She has implied she thinks corporations (or her husband) should run the nation's economy. If corporations run the economy, they will need legal and political power to do so. Clinton is more than willing to give it to them. The Owners own her.

Ask yourself. How often does Wall Street NOT get its way? It does not matter who suffers, even when the law is on their side. Take the situation in North Dakota at Standing Rock over the pipeline. The land Energy Transfer Partners is going through was given by treaty to the tribe. Still, they are going through it because the Owners want it. It should be no surprise, considering they are backed by banks such as Well Fargo. President Trump also has money invested, so he naturally came out in favor of it. What the Owners want, they get. The federal government has said little, including most of the politicos, you would expect to take a stand one way or another. The only ones who have not remained silent are Senator Bernie Sanders and Tulsi Goddard. I would say bless them if I believed in a god.

It shows why our economy is so messed up. Our economy has got to change. We need to create a democratic socialist economy. True, democratic socialism leans more towards government takeover of the means of production. It is done to allow more control by the people and to provide for the people. I prefer Bernie Sander's version, which is, in fact, social democracy. Social democracy seeks to reform capitalism in a way where the economy is regulated with the people in mind. Both philosophies look to peacefully transform societies.

I think we should use a hybrid of these two systems as the basic model. We should nationalize the enormous corporations that involve energy, food production, and the environment. These corporations have a direct impact on our lives. The power that we use, the food we eat, the water and the air we breathe. Companies should not have that much control over human beings. We cannot allow Nestle to buy up Lake Michigan's aquifer water so they can bottle it while Flint, MI, must use poisoned water. Other corporations, like automakers and banks, must no longer receive bailouts from taxpayers. There is no such thing as "too big to fail."

Let them fail. Why should the taxpayer be responsible for saving these huge entities? It's not like they would help us if we got into trouble. They would just foreclose. Besides, capitalism, like nature, abhors a vacuum. If banks or other companies fail, smaller ones will take their place. Large companies like Wal-Mart and McDonalds, who send their employees to government programs like food stamps because they don't want to pay them a living wage, must be cut off. Why should the taxpayer pay for their employees? Companies like this should be forced to pay back every cent to both their workers and to the government if they go out of business, fine. Better-run companies will replace them. We also need to start sending these bankers and crooked CEOs to jail. Iceland did that just a few years ago. Iceland can do it, and we cannot?

Another measure we can take to protect American workers is to stop the practice of companies closing their manufacturing facilities in this country and shipping those jobs to foreign lands. It was done recently by Carrier, the heating and cooling equipment builder. The corporation closed its factory in Indiana and sent those jobs to Mexico, putting at least 1100 out of work. These are the jobs Donald Trump claimed he saved by threatening to impose huge fines on the company. Bernie Sanders has made similar proposals to fine or tax departing companies. I would go further. I suggest we not only levy fines against these corporations but ban them from doing business in the United States. The corporations will no doubt threaten to close all their operations down, potentially putting thousands of workers on unemployment. I say, let them. It will allow smaller companies to expand and take their place with plenty of experienced people to fill the new factories. The fact is that even big companies cannot afford to lose the USA as a market. They will fall in line.

It is the point where capitalism starts coming back into the mix, let automakers go to the banks and get loans. Capitalism will still work for small business owners. We always want to promote the entrepreneurial spirit that made America great, just not the greediness. We can also address economic inequality by raising the minimum wage and making the labor board stronger so people will no longer need to turn to unions. Most unions tend to be corrupt and generally in bed with the Owners. They cannot be trusted. When they were first formed, I'm sure it was with the best interest of the worker in mind. It is no longer the case. We have government regulations for the proper conducting of business and labor relations. We need more of them, and they need to be made stronger.

A new wrinkle has been introduced. There is a new desire by the Owners to automate everything. A close friend told me she is working on automation for her firm, which is a significant company. She is working herself out of her job. Because of the fight for a $15 minimum wage, Owners like Andrew Puzder, CEO of Hardee's and Carl's JR and now former Secretary of Labor candidate, plans to automate his restaurants fully. He intends to replace personnel with ordering kiosks and other machines. What he does not realize is if he (and other fast-food restaurants) does not want to pay his workers' fair wages and would instead replace them, who's going to patronize his business? When workers make a decent wage, they tend to spend most of it, which aids the economy.

Furthermore, since these people are not wealthy, they will most likely go to the type of restaurants Mr. Puzder owns. He is cutting off his nose to spite his face. Jobs like these were the way inexperienced workers and others could put themselves into the job market. Now, we will have even more people who will not be able to support themselves. We are going to have another reason to do what must be done, reduce the population.

Recently, there have been calls for a universal basic income. The idea is everyone receives a set amount, whether they are working or not, ensuring they can meet their basic needs. If they want or have a job, they can make money over that. I remember seeing a film about this sort of thing when I was a kid on TV. It was one of those film shorts from the 1930s or 1940s they would show before the main feature. There was a man in a city looking for other people. There is no one in either the factories or the offices. Eventually, he meets another man (a Doodles Weaver type) who explains where everyone is. They are all at the beach! The man told him nobody works anymore because everybody had become technocrats. Automation had utterly taken over, so there was no need for anyone to accomplish.

It now appears we are heading in that direction to some extent. We can pass more and more of our tasks to increasingly sophisticated machines. However, it does not follow that, after going through all the trouble and expense to automate, the Owners are going to be willing to provide a basic income, through taxes, to anybody. After all, wasn't that the whole point of automating in the first place? To eliminate the need for workers, you should pay? I also do not think the average person who is working would want to support those who do not. I wouldn't. Many people don't like doing that now. Others, like myself, don't mind helping people who are on welfare and other such programs, but even we do not want people to stay in them in perpetuity.

To make the economy better reduce the population. The capitalist way of thinking is to expand markets continually. The best way to grow is to create more people. That way of thinking must come to an end. Why not gear an economy for a much smaller population? The economy and everything else will be proportionate to the lower number of people. There will no longer be much growth, but there will be sustainability. There will be more resources, less pressure on the environment without the pollution associated with large numbers of people. Society will become a happier place.

Why Republicans (and the Owners) Think Like They Do

In the Ayn Rand novel *Atlas Shrugged*, protagonist John Galt borrows a car from his friend Midas Mulligan to give heroine Dagny Taggart the grand tour of his Atlantis, referred to affectionately as "Galt's Gulch" by the inhabitants. Only Galt doesn't borrow the car; he *rents* it. He only pays twenty-five cents, probably far less than someone could rent a car for even in the 1950s when the book was written. However, this seemingly minor action boils down all of Rand's philosophy of capitalism to one point. As Galt explains to Dagny, everything must be paid or traded. This idea made sense to Rand. Everything has value; therefore, everything is for sale and must be paid for. If Galt simply borrowed the car that would be perceived as a charitable act by Midas Mulligan. Ayn Rand hated altruism.

Why is this relevant? It is because Rand has been the most significant influence on the Republican Party. One would think it would be Adam Smith, who laid the blueprint for Capitalism in his 1776 work *The Wealth of Nations,* but this is not the case. Ayn Rand permeates the entire philosophy of the party. Former Chairman of the Federal Reserve Alan Greenspan was part of Rand's inner circle. Soon to be former Speaker of the House, Paul Ryan required everyone who worked for him to read *Atlas Shrugged.* The book is a fun read if you look at it taking place in an alternative universe, one where industrialists are honest and noble, but it certainly is not a manual on how to run a country. Randian philosophy informs Republican governing strategies. You undoubtedly have heard of the Libertarian Party. It couldn't be any more Rand if she found it herself. Luminaries such as the Koch brothers are among their ranks. One of the brothers, David Koch, ran for president as a Libertarian in 1980. They were once considered the idiots of the political world, but their mindset carries much weight in Republican circles. Libertarians may not be able to get elected themselves, but their goals control Republicans.

Let us look at two recent instances. Recently (as of this writing), Republicans voted to reject internet privacy. By doing so, this allows your data to be bought and sold. Your personal information, the sites you visit, your shopping preferences, everything is now available for purchase. You don't want that information to be sold? Too bad, you have no say in it.

The second instance is Trump's administration's attempt to repeal and replace Obamacare. Although the American Health Care Act (aka Trumpcare) was already doomed to fail, Paul Ryan kept working on it. He especially wanted the House Freedom Caucus to sign off on it, figuring this would give it a better chance of passing since the caucus is highly influential in the Republican Party.

Unfortunately for Ryan, the Freedom Caucus proved to be even more Randian than he is. They wanted to remove benefits like hospitalization, ambulance services, emergency room services, and just about everything else you would expect health insurance to cover. Even many Republicans were against this bill. Not because they cared about the people who would be hurt by it, but they knew people were already rising against them. They knew if they repealed Obamacare without a better replacement, their constituents would come after them with torches.

The truth is Republicans have no interest in replacing the Affordable Care Act. They only want to repeal it. Republicans are not interested in doing anything that helps people. It is why they are determined to gut or flat out eliminate agencies and programs like the Environmental Protection Agency, the Department of Education, Public Broadcasting, Meals on Wheels, and so on. You see, to Republicans and their Owners, such agencies and programs do not add to their bottom line. In the case of regulatory agencies, they hurt it. Social programs might help people raise themselves out of poverty. The arts may inspire people to be more than they are now. Therefore, these things are useless to the Republican mindset. To them, people only serve two purposes; be the labor that produces goods and services and be the consumers that purchase those goods and services.

The one area where Republicans do not mind spending money is the military. We currently spend more than the next nine countries combined. President Trump wants to add another $54 billion to that. Why? The military is famous for being wasteful with money, such as paying $10,000 for one hammer or $20,000 for a toilet seat. If anything, we should be cutting the military budget. I think this might speak to the Republican/Owner fear someone might come along to take their money away from them. They figure they earned it, it's theirs, and nobody is going to take it from them. Maybe it is not a foreign power they fear, perhaps that massive military exists because they fear us.

Religion also bears responsibility for the Republican/Owner way of thinking. It is religion that creates the mindset certain people are chosen by their god to rule and be fruitful. They believe the world was set up with a particular order, and they are at the head of it. This delusion also justifies their sense of privilege.

Once again, we come back to Ayn Rand. Republicans and their Owners were greedy long before Rand came along, but Rand was the one who said, as others have noted, that it is ok to be a greedy scumbag. She was the voice of Capitalism gone mad. When I was younger, it was not uncommon to see young men and women wearing T-shirts that sported Rand's famous tagline from *Atlas Shrugged*: "Who is John Galt?" It turns out for many of them; it was themselves.

Crime and Punishment

Crime. People worry about it. This fear is especially real if you live in a high crime area. Politicians are always going on about how they are going to get tough on crime, but they never really seem to, do they? The fact is crime has been going down for decades. Thanks to better investigating techniques, policing, and a better economy, crime is at its lowest level in twenty years.

There are causes of crime. The main factor is economic. People become desperate when the economy, at least the economy that surrounds them locally, falls apart. Also, if people are poorly educated, either because of bad schools or their own laziness, they will gravitate towards crime. People must feed themselves and possibly families. If they have no honest way to make money, what are they supposed to do? Education is also critical. The more intelligent someone is, the less likely they will turn criminal—fun fact: The Atheist population in prison is only 0.07 percent.

The logical solution is to create jobs. We need to force the large corporations to build factories, warehouses, retail stores, and other services into these crumbling neighborhoods. Ensure their safety by hiring more police. When people who might turn to crime can get honest, decent-paying jobs, they will stay upright, and crime will go down even further.

Another cause of crime is attitudes. When people get the idea (sometimes from the media) that it is cool to be a criminal, it's fun to take what you want instead of working for it. Maybe it is also fun to hurt people, perhaps kill them. Maybe the wiring in their head is messed up. Perhaps some people prefer to be stupid. In any case, they are bad for society and must be stopped. Such tendencies usually appear in high school, but sometimes in middle school or even grammar school. I suggest we temporarily remove these children from the larger body of students and give them intense ethical instruction. It may require removing them from their parents if they are too weak to aid in the direction or be the cause of the specific attitude problem. The goal is to change the child's perspective. This instruction can go on until they finish high school if necessary. Furthermore, there will be no more quitting of high school. Students who have situations where they might have to help support their families will receive help so they won't have to leave school.

If people still insist on committing crimes, they will be punished. One pure, beautiful punishment. The death penalty. We are no more trying to reform criminals. That was the purpose of the school programs. If someone has reached adulthood with criminal intentions, they have decided their fate. No more need for most prisons except to incarcerate those awaiting trial. This action will also end the for-profit prison system. Trials will be speedy, efficient, and utilize all investigation methods, including DNA. DNA testing can also be used to exonerate those already in prison, as I have suggested elsewhere. Everyone involved will be investigated to make sure no one has any preconceived prejudice of the accused. If found innocent, it is with the understanding they can be brought to trial again if new evidence surfaces. I know this will anger those who buy into the concept you cannot be tried twice for the same crime. Why not? If someone is guilty, but the proof was not found until after the trial, why should that person get off scot-free? Once someone is found guilty, they will not be allowed to languish for years or decades. They must be put to death within one month unless there is a good reason to postpone it. If we follow this, crime may become practically non-existent.

The best thing we can do, as hinted at earlier, executes all proven criminals currently in prison. You cannot reform them. They had their shot. True, many did suffer the conditions I described earlier, but we must draw the line somewhere. Is it fair? Perhaps not. Life is not always balanced.

This way will eliminate repeat offenders. We can finally create a society free of crime.

Nutjob Reprobate Assassins

Recently, the National Rifle Association held its convention in Dallas, TX. Gun owners came from all over the country to celebrate the Second Amendment. As usual, with meetings, local businesses stood to have a nice uptick in their profits. As reported by the Washington Post, the owner of Ellen's Diner, Joe Groves, had made a decision. Groves, a supporter of the 2nd Amendment himself, printed on his diner's receipts a pledge to donate part of the proceeds to "implementing reasonable and effective gun regulations."

The NRA caught wind of this and tweeted a photo of the receipt. Groves modified the receipt to include "citizens' 2nd Amendment rights," but the NRA had already pounced. They advised conventioneers to avoid the restaurant. The diner's social media pages were swamped with posts. While many were approving, others were hostile. Ellen's Diner got calls threatening "to shoot the place up." During the convention, the diner enjoyed a 26% increase in business. It allowed Joe Groves to give Moms Demand Action, a group formed after the Sandy Hook shooting, a check for $15,000.

Mr. Groves was attempting to address a significant problem in our society. The question of mass murder. Granted, in theory, mass murder, defined as the killing of four or more people, can be accomplished by different means. One could use poison, a bomb, or even a van, as happened recently in Toronto. Most killings, however, take place by using guns. It's simple to kill with a gun. Just point and shoot. Thanks to the easy availability of assault rifles with no background checks, you can kill more people than ever.

What makes someone want to kill large groups of people? There are many potential causes. The United States is a country that emphasizes achievement. We have a culture that equates success with fame. Many of these shooters are losers who have never accomplished anything, and they want to be famous. Maybe they were bullied. Perhaps they were ignored. Maybe women wouldn't have sex with them, as was the cause behind two of the recent shootings by "incels." It could only be they just got that spanking new automatic rifle and wanted to try it out. They had to know things would not end well for them. They would rather die (often by their own hand), or they would be captured.

After the shooting at Parkland High School, the student survivors organized a march on Washington. It was a massive march with several satellite marches around the country. The young activists called for background checks and the banning of assault rifles. Reasonable measures. Gun nuts jumped on them. Some threatened physical violence against them, kids! One of the student leaders, Emma Gonzales, had a photo of herself tearing up a target photoshopped into her tearing up the Constitution.

The United States has more mass shootings than any other country. Those shootings have only increased in recent years. Before 2011, a mass shooting occurred approximately once every 200 days. From 2011-2014, that number went up to once roughly every 64 days. Now it seems even higher. The United States has the highest rate of gun ownership in the world per capita. Coming in at a distant second is Yemen. Guns are too easy to get in this country. If your rifle does not already shoot enough bullets, you can buy a bump stock, which allows you to shoot a semi-automatic at an automatic rate. My question is, *why* do you *need* such a deadly weapon?

You cannot hunt with it. What are you going to do? Splatter that deer's head all over the forest? Good luck hanging that on your wall. Home protection? Maybe against a bear charging towards your house, but it strikes me a rifle of any type would be too unwieldy to use indoors in most situations. A pistol would be better. Do you want to protect yourself from the government? You're kidding, right? Even if you have multiple weapons (as were used in more than half of the mass shootings in the US), what are you going to do against a tank? They could just drop a bomb on you. Why does anyone who is not in the military need military-type assault weapons?

The Second Amendment of the Constitution. The language of it is pretty straightforward:

"A well-regulated Militia, being necessary to the security of a free State, the right of the people to keep and bear Arms, shall not be infringed."

A keyword is a *militia.* The Oxford dictionaries define a militia as "a military force that is raised from the civil population to supplement a regular army in an emergency." It was expected the citizenry would rise and defend the country if attacked or aid in some other manner. What eventually happened is these state militias evolved into the National Guard. There is no longer a need for state militias. It seems to be the "right of the people to bear arms" referred to people who actually serve in the militia. Former Supreme Court Justice John Paul Stevens suggested, in a Washington Post piece from April 11, 2014, the Second Amendment could be "fixed" by adding five words to it: "...the right of the people to keep and bear Arms *when serving in the Militia* shall not be infringed."

Another relevant term is *well regulated*. Militias were trained and commanded by actual military officers. The militias of a country would form a regiment. It was necessary since the United States only maintained a minimal federal army. State militias were vital to the safety of the country. We no longer have well-regulated militias. Now we have groups of gun-toting losers who play soldier. Often, they are white supremacists, wannabe Confederate rebels, or skinhead Nazi types. David Koresh's Branch Davidians shared much of the same mindset. They are extremely dangerous. There is a reason the government keeps tabs on them.

The common thread is they share a distrust, fear, and hatred of government. At the time of the writing of the Constitution, when all guns could only shoot one bullet, there were concerns that a standing federal army might try to usurp power. It was even a concern of James Madison, the author of the Constitution. He believed state militias could keep the military in check. The self-appointed defenders of freedom worry their guns are going to be taken from them. It is a fear the NRA strokes. In my personal opinion, however, I think the main attraction is that guns give a feeling of power to those who see themselves as powerless. Maybe they aren't intelligent, wealthy, or even good looking, but they can kill. It makes them feel powerful and vital.

The National Rifle Association. In this country, one cannot talk about guns without talking about the NRA. Rich and powerful, they are the organ for gun owners' access to politicians and legislation. Initially founded by Civil War veterans Col. William C. Church and Gen. George Wingate, the NRA promoted good marksmanship and gun safety. They have worked with the US Fish and Wildlife Service to promote conservation. During WW II, the NRA aided the war effort by creating training materials and encouraged members to serve as plant and home guards. Somewhere along the line, this once helpful organization lost its way. It began pursuing a technically correct but narrow interpretation of the 2nd Amendment. They want everyone to have access to any kind of gun they wish. It does not matter the age, mental health, or criminal status of the person. They don't want background checks. It seems like they don't even want gun training anymore. They just want everybody to have a gun (or several) no matter what. To this end, they funnel vast amounts of money into Washington through their NRA Foundation, which they established in 1990. They give money to whoever supports their policies.

They do appear to prefer Republicans. Perhaps this is because Republicans tend to be conservative. A love for guns is seen as a traditional trait. Speaker of the House Paul Ryan is the current champ of NRA donations at $171,977.000. The top fifteen beneficiaries of NRA donations are Republicans. In 2016, Republicans received $5,900,000 in contributions while the Democrats only got a paltry $106,000, according to Politico. We've always known politicians are for sale. Now we know human life is not essential to them at all.

Oddly enough, I once had two guests on my old cable access TV show who were liberal lawyers. They both admitted they had guns. In their case, it was for their protection. I got a concealed carry permit when I moved to Georgia because I feared, as both a somewhat liberal type and an Atheist, I would find myself targeted. It turned out my fear was unsubstantiated. I never bought a gun, but I have made peace with weapons. I have no problem with firearms for personal protection, target shooting, or hunting, even though I could never go hunting myself. Too soft-hearted. I still have no use for the NRA. Unfortunately, the current state of this country negates any severe talk of banning firearms.

A recent poll by John Hopkins, published in the New England Journal of Medicine, found 89% of those who responded, including 75% who are NRA members, support background checks. Surveys by Pew Research Center and Gallup had similar results. They also supported disallowing people with recent alcohol or drug offenses to purchase guns and jail time (unfortunately, not much jail time) for gun sellers who sell to people not legally allowed to have guns. Most people, even some NRA members, want to ban assault weapons as well. These seem to be reasonable precautions. Why does the NRA ignore their members?

As I researched this essay, some disturbing questions came to mind. What if the NRA and the gun fanatics are right about the government becoming totalitarian? Previously, this suggestion would have been absurd. Now we have a wannabe dictator for president. He enjoys much support. People seem to want an authoritarian in charge. Ironically, the gun owners and the NRA support him. They help him despite the fact one of the first things dictators do is take away peoples' guns. Obama never tried this even though the NRA accused him of it several times. We want to make assault weapons illegal. In a sane world, that would not be a problem, but what if Trump succeeds in turning this country fascist? We would have to become an "underground" like they had in Nazi Germany. Would the NRA and the self-styled militias join us in fighting Trump, or would they ally themselves further with him and seek only to take away our guns? These are questions we should ask gun owners and ourselves. I don't know the answers. What would we do?

A Foolish Conceit

I have white privilege. I did not ask for it. I do not want it. Still, I have it, and I'm stuck with it. It is offensive to me and the principles I have tried to live by all my life. It is against Humanist philosophy and just plain decency.

White privilege, as I'm sure you are aware, is an intangible benefit bestowed on white people solely for being white. Most white people may not care or even notice it. However, if you are not white, white privilege plays into your life in subtle, overt, and sometimes devastating ways. It should not be surprising. What it all comes down to, no matter what euphemism you call it by, it is everyday old racism.

However, the word racism does not cover it all, mainly because the term is not broad enough. According to Merriam-Webster, the word was not even used until the Twentieth Century. Although, as Merriam-Webster also points out, the concept could be around long before the actual term for it came about. For me, racism only describes distrust and hatred towards those of another "race." An idea I also have trouble with because, to me, there is only *one* race, the human race.

What humans perceive as different races are just variations within the species, differences such as skin color, the shape of eyes, and so on are no more significant than eye or hair color. Is anyone hated because they have red hair? To my mind, the term racist is useless and illogical.

The more useful term would be prejudice. The word describes not only the attitude cited above but all negative attitudes towards human beings. It includes the hatred towards women, LBGT, older people, poor people, those from other countries, other religions, as well as people of a different color. Remember, people can even be prejudiced against others within their genetic group. For instance, toward the end of the Nineteenth Century and into the Twentieth, Irish people were the target of discrimination because they were perceived as being violent drunkards, or in the modern Middle East, there is the endless conflict between Jews and Arabs despite their genetic similarity.

Let's look at how prejudice is defined. The first definition concerns its use in jurisprudence, which does not involve us here. It is the second definition that is pertinent to this discussion. Again, from Merriam-Webster:

a (1): preconceived judgment or opinion

(2): an adverse opinion or leaning formed without just grounds or before sufficient knowledge
b: an instance of such judgment or opinion
c: an irrational attitude of **hostility** directed against an individual, a group, a race, or their supposed characteristics

Ok, so now we have a handle on what I see as the proper term. The next question is, why do humans think like this? I see a big part of it is because of religion. Since religions are tribal, they institutionalize prejudice and hate. The more fundamentalist the faith, the worse the bias is. Anyone outside of the religious group is to be mistrusted if not outright hated. Even within the religions themselves, different denominations often hate each other. It has caused a lot of bloody history. Disputes over land and such can usually be worked out, but when people fight over beliefs, it is more primal.

Still, even if religion never existed, we would have prejudice. I would argue it would be much less pervasive, but it would always be here. Humans are tribal. It may have been a survival technique to mistrust anyone outside the group. Perhaps that is part of being human. There no reason to think we cannot overcome it. You might argue I am prejudiced. As you have no doubt gathered, I do not care for the religious. Because of that, you could lump me into the "haters." I would argue no. I bear no malice against the faithful because of any physical trait, country of origin, or economic status. My objection is only to their belief systems, which can be objectively determined as incorrect and dangerous. History and current events vindicate me on this. However, I have no problem with the religious so long as they do not try to push their beliefs on me or society.

The next question, of course, is what we can do about it? To me, the most sensible approach is education. Perhaps we need in-school instruction for something children should have learned at home. It is another reason the public school is so essential, socialization. Children (and people in general) need to be brought together so they can learn from each other and that their differences do not amount to much. Home-schooled children and private schools often keep children isolated to their own social, religious, or economic group. What to do about these children I have no idea. Suggestions? As for children in public schools, we can apply principles from another essay in this book, "What About the Children?" We can test their social skills. If need be, remove them from school for more intensive instruction. If their parents are the problem, remove them from their parents, either temporarily or permanently.

These are things we must do. Hatred is its once again rearing its ugly head. The presidency of Donald Trump has emboldened bigots. Trump, a known bigot who has been sued many times for discriminating against potential tenants in his apartment buildings, became president by playing to peoples' prejudices. When neo-Nazis and other white supremacists marched in Charlottesville, VA, in 2017, Trump defended them by saying there were "good people, on both sides." A counter-protester, 32-year-old Heather Heyer, was killed when one of the supremacists drove his car into the crowd.

I suppose I feel strongly about this because my mother, who was Jewish (although not observant), told me she didn't let people know she was Jewish because people were often anti-Semitic. When my stepdad once jokingly referred to her as his "little Jewish lady," she shot him the dirtiest look I had ever seen her give, and my mom was known for her dirty looks.

If we do not want to have more Charlottesvilles and Waffle House shooters, we have got to put an end to these attitudes and behavior. People of goodwill must step up, speak out, ridicule, and, if necessary, fight both the hate and the haters.

I remember once seeing a 1950s rendition of Superman telling kids that schools, like our country, are made up of Americans of different races, religions, and national origins, and prejudice was wrong. In a more recent controversial storyline, Superman protected people being victimized by a gun-toting bigot type. Who better than Superman to the point that out to kids? After all, doesn't Superman stand for truth, justice, and the American Way? To me, that should be the American Way.

What's the Deal Already?

On January 21ˢᵗ, 2017, the first Woman's March was held. Originally intended to be just a march on Washington DC, it quickly grew into a worldwide phenomenon, ultimately drawing over six million women in over 600 cities. It was the most massive protest march in the history of the world. It was focused on a plethora of social issues of concern to everyone, but perhaps particularly women—equality, human rights, freedom of religion, reproductive rights, LGBTQ rights, and others.

Women were adorned in their "pussy hats." Hats made of pink material with ears like a cat's, also a reference to sexist comments by Donald Trump in 2005. "And when you're a star, they let you do it." "You can do anything, Grab 'em by the pussy. Anything." Women took to the streets to protest not only for the issues mentioned earlier but to protest against President Trump, who indeed has not become any more enlightened since then.

While it is true, Trump is a sexist pig and represents an immense danger to women's rights and the rights of everyone. One question remains. Why didn't women do this years ago? Most men have always been sexist pigs. Trump is perceived as being more so, but he is not. He is more or less representative of the men who think this way, including many in governments around the world. Unfortunately, the world continues to believe in this destructive patriarchal way.

In Islamic countries, these attitudes are particularly cruel and dangerous. Driven by their barbaric religion, these countries allow no human rights for women. They must be covered from head to foot in burkas; they cannot leave the house without a male relative, the man rules the family, and in most of these countries, women cannot even drive a car. Moreover, any perceived impropriety is dealt with harshly, often by murder. These are so-called "honor killings." Interesting term, since these men have no honor. It has been known to happen even in the United States, where one would think they came to escape such horrors.

While not as extreme, horrors persist in this country because of <u>our</u> barbaric religion. Well, yours, not mine. Women are still basically second-class citizens. They have had to fight for everything they have obtained. Even so, many men would love to turn the clock back. Some of it is, of course, male ego. We have a lot of it. I think the most significant factor is how boys are raised and view the world. They are taught (consciously or subconsciously) the world is in the order of a hierarchy, God, king, men, women, and children. While it is true children need to be guided by adults, there is no reason whatsoever why the top should not be shared equally by men and women. No need for God at all.

An interesting note; early societies were once matriarchal and worshipped female gods. Most likely, this was because women could give birth, literately create life, which men could not. It brings me to another point. Since men cannot give birth, what business is it of theirs if women want to control their bodies? Why do men (and quite a few women as well) want to force motherhood on those who do not want it? Of course, this is due to the influence of religious cults. The Bible teaches "be fruitful and multiply." This concept might have made some sense when numbers were relatively small, and you would need as many people as possible to defend yourself from enemies or work the farm. There are no barbarians at the gate now (if you exclude religionists themselves), so there is no practical need for this anymore. Like religion, this is all about control. Men, either through nature or nurture, seek to control all within their sphere. This desire also includes women. It does not matter whether there is a family connection or not. To this mindset, *all* women are theirs to control.

I also think there is a fear, which men won't admit that women could do jobs better than they can. When I started working in warehouses forty years ago, the only women you might see worked on a line doing simple assembly. You would never see a woman on a forklift or other such equipment. At my last job, there were many women on this equipment. Perhaps roughly about the same number as men. Back in the day, the only positions, for the most part, women seemed suited for were teachers, nurses, secretaries, wives, and mothers.

Interestingly, this all changed during World War II. Since men were off fighting the war, women had to work the jobs previously done by those men. Unfortunately, once the war was over, women were forced back into the kitchen. At the new Westmont Station apartments in New Jersey, site of the former Curtis-Wright complex, there is a statue of Rosie the Riveter, the symbol of these heroines.

While the status of women has improved, there is still much to do. Women again don't make the same money as men do, even if they do the same job. This pay inequity is justified by men because "they don't have families to support." What? Of course, women have families to support. Very often, they are the only breadwinner in the family, even if they are married. What about single mothers? It is just one more rationalization to keep women "in their place."

Now it is true there are some differences between men and women. Men tend to have greater upper body strength. Women can endure more pain (try having a baby sometime.) Men seem to be better at "figuring stuff out," basically engineering, but women tend to do better in mathematics. Of course, these are just generalizations, but what they should tell us is this should not be a competition.

The good news is that not all men are sexist. Some men marched for women's suffrage at the beginning of the Twentieth Century. Men are growing more sensitive to the needs of women. We cannot appreciate everything they go through simply because we are not women, but we can understand on an intellectual basis.

Both sexes have much to offer that complement each other. So what's the deal with this stupid war against women? Where is the logic in this? I must confess I was pretty chauvinistic when I was a kid. I didn't know any better. It was when I learned about Humanism and Atheism that I saw the error of my ways. If I could grow, so can other men. C'mon guys.

Inexcusable!

My niece hinted to me; I should not write this essay. After all, as a man, what could I possibly know about the subject? In a way, she is correct. I can only deal with this on an intellectual level. This sort of thing has never happened to me. There may be a handful of men in the world who have experienced this but not me. I still feel I need to add my voice. We *have* to know. All men must know about this so that we can prevent it in the future.

I am speaking about sexual harassment. You know, the thing that has been in the news so much lately? It's not like this is a recent phenomenon. Sexual harassment has always existed throughout human history. It is only recently the subject has been receiving the full attention it deserves. It is due, of course, to the Me-Too movement. Women are tired of being pushed around. It was one of the primary motivators of the Women's March. Don't you think an issue like this is essential, considering it affects half the population of the planet?

Sexual harassment may be defined as unwanted sexual attention and advances towards an individual. Generally, but not always, the victims are women. Although harassment can take place anywhere, it is most common in the workplace. This behavior is because workers feel they must submit to their supervisors. The harassers think the same way. Workers must bow to them. If the perpetrator is a supervisor, they have at least some measure of control over the worker. Since they have, in effect, power over someone, they think they have the right to demand sexual favors from them. An employee may not feel able to turn down their boss since he/she can determine their pay structure or even their continued employment. The Equal Employment Opportunity Commission (EEOC) defines sexual harassment in the workplace. I am using Wikipedia's condensing of this definition to spare you the "legalese":

Unwelcome sexual advances, requests for sexual favors, or other verbal or physical conduct of a sexual nature when:
1. Submission to such conduct was made either explicitly or implicitly a term or condition of an individual's employment,
2. Submission to or rejection of such conduct by an individual was used as the basis for employment decisions affecting such individual, or
3. Such conduct has the purpose or effect of unreasonably interfering with an individual's work performance or creating

an intimidating, hostile, or offensive working environment.

Harassers do not necessarily need to be a supervisor. A co-worker can do the same thing. They can continuously badger their fellow employee with requests for dates, etc. They might not even realize they are doing something wrong. Back in the day, it was simply referred to as "coming on too strong." While workplace harassment is the most common, harassment can happen elsewhere too. Probably the next most common situation would be social interaction. It may occur when a friend decides they want to be something more. Again, following the "too strong" scenario, the harasser may not even realize what they are doing. They are doing it nonetheless.

If someone is in a bar or "at the club," they know there is always the possibility somebody will solicit them for sex in this environment that is a reasonable thing to do and expect one to do. However, if the attention is unwelcome, unrelenting, and/or leads to bullying, it becomes unacceptable. While some men have trouble accepting this because they cannot believe a woman would not welcome their advances, no means no! Just pick your ego up off the floor and quietly walk away. Would you want your mother or sister treated this way? If anyone ever did this to my niece, they would meet the business end of my fist.

As you might suspect, this sexual pressure places high stress upon its victims. It leads to terrible effects, which include but not limited to: loss of self-esteem, humiliation, damage to existing relationships, difficulty in the workplace, and loss of trust. There is often a backlash against the victim, not only from the perpetrator but others, even fellow employees. Very often, they become the accused because they are seen as "wanting it" or because they want attention. These incidents can destroy a person's life.

Over the years, sexual harassment has been defined by several courts, including the United States Supreme Court. Various cases helped codify the legal definitions of the term. Furthermore, sexual harassment is now seen as a violation of the Civil Rights Act of 1964

It brings us to the Me-Too movement. Founded in 2006 by Tarana Burke. The intention was, according to their website, "to help survivors of sexual violence, particularly young women of color from low wealth communities, find pathways to healing." The movement soon grew and expanded to include all people who had been harassed. The campaign exploded when actress Alyssa Milano encouraged the use of the hashtag *#Me Too* to spread awareness of the extent of sexual harassment. Women from all walks of life began coming forward. The movement has now spread worldwide.

In the United States, the most well-known stories of sexual harassment come from the world of entertainment and politics. Celebrities such as Reese Witherspoon, Gwyneth Paltrow, and Angelina Jolie told tales of harassment by producers and studio heads. Ultimately this led to resignations and firings. Two high profile cases stand out. Harvey Weinstein, a co-founder of both Miramax and the Weinstein Company and producer or executive producer of such films as *Shakespeare In Love* and *The Crying Game,* is, so far, the biggest name accused. The "casting couch" has existed since the earliest days of Hollywood. Weinstein seems to have taken it to a whole new level. Over eighty women have accused Weinstein of misconduct, and some have accused him of actual rape. As a result, Weinstein is being sued; he was expelled from the Motion Picture Academy of Arts and Sciences and was stripped of various honors. He also was recently indicted for rape and sex crime charges.

The second case was Bill O'Reilly, "political commentator" and all-around blowhard for Fox News. O'Reilly, the phony populist famous for his program *The O'Reilly Factor,* found himself in the no spin zone when he also was accused by women of harassment. The New York Times reported in April 2017 O'Reilly and Fox News had settled five lawsuits since 2002. When this information came out, O'Reilly's show lost advertisers, more than half of them. Roger Ailes, the Fox News chairman, could no longer help O'Reilly since he was dismissed over his allegations. Before much longer, O'Reilly would follow Ailes. He was let go by the end of April. I could go on about more Hollywood types such as Bill Cosby, but I want to keep this pithy.

The New York Attorney General Eric Schneiderman, a well-known liberal Democrat and defender of women's rights (he sued Harvey Weinstein), found himself in hot water when the New Yorker magazine published an article in which four former lovers accused Schneiderman of violence against them. He tried to dodge, saying: "In the privacy of intimate relationships, I have engaged in role-playing and other consensual sexual activity. I have not assaulted anyone. I have never engaged in nonconsensual sex, which is a line I would not cross." Schneiderman resigned three hours after the magazine hit the newsstands.

Al Franken, the senator from Minnesota and former cast member of *Saturday Night Live,* was a liberal darling. He authored books. Franken served in the senate from 2009 to 2018. He would still be in the Senate today. He, too, was caught misbehaving. He was not violent or even threatening, but he acted in a juvenile manner that undermined his credibility and destroyed his government career. In 2006, while they were on a USO tour, Franken forcibly kissed a woman named Leeann Tweeden. There was also a photo taken of Franken pretending to fondle (not touch) her breasts while she was asleep.

Along with other incidents of inappropriate touching (although nothing like Donald Trump) ruined him. He did apologize, but the damage was done. No doubt, Franken thought he was having innocent fun. The "boys will be boys" mentality.

None of this surprises me. It most likely does not surprise you either. Harassment happens everywhere. In the military, it happens more than in civilian life. In churches, the repositories of humanity's sins, two women started their own hashtag, *#Church Too,* and evangelical women started *#SilenceIsNotSpiritual.*

The big shocker for me personally is when two famous Atheists were on the receiving end of accusations. The first was Lawrence Krauss. Krauss, a theoretical physicist, and cosmologist is the author of several books, including the popular *The Physics of Star Trek.* He refers to himself as an Antitheist, as I do. He publicly debated religionists and was a leading voice for reason. According to

Buzzfeed, in 2006, Krauss allegedly tried to force himself on Melody Hensley. Stories about Krauss had been going on for years but were suppressed by Krauss's supporters. They came to light in a February 2018 article in Buzzfeed. It is where I first learned about them. I guess Krauss will not be doing a cameo on the *Big Bang Theory*, Mayim Bialik would go ballistic and rightfully so.

An interesting side note: after reading the article, I took to the comment section. A short time later, a Christian, Dick Clearly, took me to task on his *Viewpoint* blog. Not because I made a couple of typos (I don't always proof-read when I'm mad, and I didn't think someone would be quoting me) but instead asked how harassment would not be ok since I said there are no morals in Atheism. It is not what I said, of course. What I said was (typo corrected): "I have no morality myself. Morality is arbitrary rules made up by old men to control the sex lives of human beings, particularly women. I have ethics, which tells you what's right." He accused me of being inconsistent, but he has no problem with the constant abuses (sexual and otherwise) churches commit. Being just a little hypocritical, aren't we Dick?

Gut punch #2 came when David Silverman, president of American Atheists and author of *Fighting God: An Atheist Manifesto for a Religious*

World, was terminated. Silverman had done good things. Silverman did the Atheist billboards during Christmas and managed to "herd cats" to create the Reason Rally. The Reason Rally was the largest gathering of Atheists ever. I admired Silverman even though he and I never cared much for each other personally. Three women have alleged that Silverman tried to push himself on them using his position to influence them. Reportedly he also appointed a woman to a post (since rescinded) because he was having a sexual relationship with her. According to Silverman's lawyer, he was in an open marriage at the time. I do hope someone told Mrs. Silverman. Former president Ed Buckner returned to serve as Interim Executive Director.

To my two fellow Atheists and anyone else who found themselves in this type of situation, I must ask: WHAT THE HELL WAS YOU THINKING??? It is inexcusable behavior. As I predicted, this is being used against us, as evidenced by my anecdote cited above. I expect this behavior from religious leaders but not from Atheists. I have been in positions of authority, but it never occurred to me I should use it to get with a woman, especially against her will. Positions of power are given to you because it has been assumed you can be trusted. You have all betrayed that trust. Assuming these allegations are correct, you deserve whatever happens to you.

Gaydar Alert!!!

I was surfing the Internet today when I came across the article "Could California Ban the Bible?" As you might suspect, this drew me in like a moth to a flame. The article described a discussion a Dr. Paul Chappell, Senior Pastor of Lancaster Baptist Church, had with Todd Starnes, Fox News' version of Alex Jones. Chappell was in a dither and panic over California Assembly Bill 2943, which, as the article put it: "...declares biblical books and Christian conferences dealing with views on homosexuality or transgenderism as fraudulent under the state's consumer fraud statute."

You might wonder how this bill somehow bans the Bible? Short answer; it doesn't. I read the bill myself. What the bill does is address the issue of fraudulent claims for goods and services. As both an example and a point, the bill addresses reparative therapy, the scam to "cure" homosexuality. The bill makes the point this so-called therapy is a sham and not supported by any legitimate psychiatric association. Therefore, it is a fraud. The more substantial part of the bill is to protect consumers from being deceived by any false claims. Nowhere in the bill does it discuss banning the Bible or any other book.

Of course, Starnes and Chappell were playing to the fear and hatred of LBGT people. The fact reparative therapy and the claims about AB 2943 are false is no obstacle to truth-challenged Fox News. It is just one more thing for Fox viewers to focus their hate on to boost their ratings and perhaps give President Trump something to tweet about.

Homosexuality has always been seen as something strange in American culture but was never a significant issue until the Stonewall riots of 1969. The gay rights movement was in its infancy when New York City police raided the Stonewall Inn on Christopher Street. Gay bars were the refuge for gay people from laws against homosexual behavior and an odd statute where you could be arrested for wearing less than three "gender appropriate" articles of clothing. Ironically, most of the gay bars at the time, including the Stonewall Inn, were owned/controlled by the Genovese crime family. For them, it was another way to make a profit. The Genovese family also bribed the local precinct, so they could ignore operating codes other bars had to adhere. You would get a watered-down drink in a place with no fire exit. Wealthier patrons would be blackmailed.

On June 28, 1969, when the police came to raid the Stonewall Inn, the people fought back. Over six days, the gay movement became galvanized. It led to the founding of organizations still around today, such as the Human Rights Campaign and PFLAG.

If you are as old as me, you remember something, or more precisely, someone who also solidified the gay movement, Anita Bryant. Bryant, a former Miss Oklahoma, singer, and concentrated orange juice huckster made headlines in the 1970s with her opposition to gay rights. She influenced anti-homosexual legislation in the state of Florida and elsewhere. Eventually, her career fell into decline, and her contract with the Florida Citrus Commission lapsed. What did she do? She started a ministry, of course!

On my old TV show, *The Free Mind*, we did a program on homosexuality. We had as guests the minister from the local Metropolitan Community Church, one of the Atlanta Freethought Society's members who were gay and the pastor of a local church, the Calvary Christian Fellowship. The Metropolitan Community Church is a nationwide network of liberal, pro-gay churches. The Calvary Christian Fellowship was a more orthodox Christian church. The Atlanta Freethought Society is (along with the Humanists of Georgia) one of the groups to which I belonged. It was a lively discussion. Throughout the program, it became clear that the only real objection to homosexuality was on religious grounds.

The Book of Leviticus in the Old Testament is the central part of the Bible that is cited against homosexually. Two verses are particular favorites:

"You shall not lie with a male as with a woman; it is an abomination."   Chapter 18 verse 22
"If a man lies with a male as with a woman, both of them have committed an abomination; they shall surely be put to death; their blood is upon them." Chapter 20 verse 13

There are other verses, as well, in both the Old and New Testaments. However, it is Leviticus that is the best known. There is also the story of Sodom (from which we get the word *sodomy*) and Gomorrah, where a mob of men demanded Lot hand over the two angels he was giving sanctuary to, so the men could *know* them. Lot, in true Biblical fashion, offered his daughters for rape instead.

We are seeing more attacks on gay people again, despite the nation and the world becoming more gay-friendly. It is part of an overall attack on anyone that is seen as different. You are probably familiar with the Westboro Baptist Church, famous for protesting of military funerals, whether they were gay or not. They carry signs declaring "God Hates Fags" as their mantra. In Nazi concentration camps, homosexuals had to wear pink triangles (Jews and others wore different badges), so they could be separated. Nazis, just like the haters of today, were influenced by their church upbringing. German soldiers wore belt buckles that declared "Gott Mit Uns" (God with Us.) As I have stated elsewhere, religion is tribal. Any deviation from their norm makes one an outsider and, therefore, an enemy. Whenever there is hate, somewhere, you will find god-worship, either directly or indirectly, in the mix.

In the age of Trump, this will continue to get worse. We have a president who delights in the way he can manipulate people for his political ambitions and pure greed. Trump has exposed an ugly part of this country many hoped was dead. It wasn't dead at all. It was just sleeping waiting for its savior. I use the word savior deliberately. Isn't Donald Trump a savior to those who value misogyny, white supremacy, and stupidity?

All this fuel a cycle of hate against a relatively small part of the population (1.6%, add 0.7% for bisexuals) that harms no one. The American Psychiatric Association and every other such association I could find does not consider homosexuality a psychological disorder. Why should anybody else? From the shooting at the

Pulse nightclub to opposition to transgender people using the restroom of their choice. Why not just make all bathrooms unisex? Why not just stop hating people? Why is what they do any skin off your nose?

My thing is, I don't care. It never occurred to me I should care about what consenting adults do in private. I don't care how many mommies Heather has. As long as people are law-abiding, peaceful, and happy, people should enjoy whatever lifestyles they choose. To borrow a line from Thomas Jefferson (he was speaking about something else, but it still applies.) "It neither picks my pocket nor breaks my leg."

No Welcome Here!

The New Colossus

Not like the brazen giant of Greek fame,
With conquering limbs astride from land to land;
Here at our sea-washed, sunset gates shall stand
A mighty woman with a torch, whose flame
Is the imprisoned lightning, and her name
Mother of Exiles. From her beacon-hand
Glows world-wide welcome; her mild eyes
command
The air-bridged harbor that twin cities frame.
"Keep, ancient lands, your storied pomp!" cries she
With silent lips. "Give me your tired, your poor,
Your huddled masses yearning to breathe free,
The wretched refuse of your teeming shore.
Send these, the homeless, tempest-tost to me,
I lift my lamp beside the golden door!"

Emma Lazarus

According to family legend, my father was born on a ship off the coast of Nova Scotia, coming to the United States. As a baby, he might not have seen, or much noticed the Statue of Liberty as he passed by it. He could not appreciate the meaning of the monument that still stands in the harbor like a lighthouse shining a beacon to the world. He certainly could not read Emma Lazarus' 1883 sonnet engraved on a plaque inside the pedestal. His parents died before they could reach their new homeland. The orphaned newborn was sent to be raised by relatives on a farm, which led to a life-long hatred of butter.

Despite the historical novel-like story of his birth, my father was not a great man. He did not rise to become a captain of industry or a statesman. He was just a plain old working stiff. He served in World War II, got married and raised a family with my mother, also the daughter of immigrants. They were nothing special, but they did work and contribute to society. Isn't that the idea?

Now, for the first time, we have a president that would like to erase those words off the Statue of Liberty. A vain, petulant child who would slam the door on those yearning to breathe free. An ignorant, bigoted fool who does not embrace the ideals of America. It is even stranger because Donald Trump's own mother was an immigrant. So was his grandfather. Two of Trump's wives were imported. However, Trump does not like immigration in general, except for maybe white people from Norway.

What is even worse is those who share his views. They have rejected what it means to be an

American. They have given in to fear, which Trump actively strokes. They fear for their jobs, which Trump actively strokes. They fear anyone different, which Trump and religion actively stroke.

Recently, Attorney General Jeff Sessions stated that anyone attempting to bring children across the border illegally would have those children taken from them. He has since made good on his threat. They are taking children away from their parents! I wouldn't even do that, and I hate children! Can you imagine anything crueler? Does this sound like the America you were raised to believe in?

It is true we must be cognitive of the world we live in now. There is a possibility that terrorists can infiltrate refugee groups. Criminals can hide among the immigrants. News flash: they always have! That is why we vet people coming into this country, including those only coming for an extended time. The 911 bombers entered the country on temporary visas but were not appropriately vetted. Three of those visas had already expired by the time of the attack.

If Trump et al. would like to cut down on immigration, we could take the approach of instead of building a wall; we make life in those countries better. After World War II, the United States created the Marshall Plan, named after the then Secretary of State. Its stated goal was to aid in the economic recovery of Europe after the war. The plan has had its distractors in recent years. They claim that the Marshall Plan served to provide markets for American businesses preventing a possible depression and remade Europe's economy after our own. To this, I say, so what? Europe was able to take the right things, make them their own, and make them better. Why not do that today? We could get other well-off countries to help as well. We do not have to bear the burden alone. If we can make these countries peaceful and economically stable, people will be happy where they are. The world will become more stable.

What Trump and his dim-witted followers do not understand is immigration adds to, not subtracts from, the vitality of our country. We are a nation of immigrants. Even those we refer to (and stole land from) as Native Americans came from somewhere else. The people who come here now are doing so to create a better life for themselves and their children, as they always have, but also many are fleeing from wars and persecution, as they always have. Americans have always helped the less fortunate people of the world. As Lazarus's poem declared, the door is open; the lamp is lifted.

The Intel on Incel

By now I'm sure everyone has heard of Incels. A month ago, it was not even on my radar screen. When I did finally hear of it, it almost sounded comical to me. It was just another silly 'movement" or cause like, the Flat Earth Society. I assumed it was another harmless group of morons with an ax to grind. My assessment was partly correct; they are morons, but they are not harmless. They want to bury their axes in peoples' heads.

Just in case the unlikely event you haven't heard of it until now, Incel refers to "involuntary celebrate." That is, as a chap I once knew would put it, a guy "who couldn't get laid in a whorehouse with a fistful of hundreds." Incels are invariably male. Where are the female incels? It is interesting because the term was coined by a woman. When she was a college student in the 1990s, a woman named Alana started an online group called "Alana's Involuntary Celibacy Project." The website was intended to be a haven for both men and women, who had difficulty finding sexual partners for whatever reason. After becoming comfortable with her identity as a lesbian, she gave the site to a stranger. Alana has since regretted the change in the meaning of the term since it is so far from what she had intended.

Incel online communities quietly grew over the next decade. They also grew from online "pick-up artist" communities. Yes, there is such a thing. They tended to become more misogynistic over time. Incels are obsessed not only from not being to obtain sex but with those who do have sex. They refer to the most attractive of these people as "Chads and Stacys." Incels have somehow convinced themselves that having sex with beautiful women is their *right*. These men believe in the superiority of the male. This attitude harkens back to our previous discussion of the perceived hierarchy of men, women, and children. Men are the rulers of the world, and as such, all women should submit to them. Women who deny them should be punished. It should not come as a surprise that many incels are also associated with alt-right movements as well.

Inevitably, any group that harbors such hatred will sooner or later turn violent. It is what happened in 2014. A young man named Eliot Rodger was responsible for murdering six people and injuring 14 more when he opened fire near the University of California, Santa Barbara campus. He also killed himself, leaving behind a 114-page manifesto and YouTube videos detailing his deranged state of mind and his plans for retribution.

To give some insight into his distorted wiring, I will cite some of Rodger's manifesto, appropriately titled *My Twisted World*, as quoted in a May 26, 2014 article by Cosmopolitan:

"I cannot kill every single female on earth, but I can deliver a devastating blow that will shake all of them to the core of their wicked hearts."

"On the day before the Day of Retribution, I will start the First Phase of my vengeance: Silently killing as many people as I can around Isla Vista by luring them into my apartment through some form of trickery,"

"The first people I would have to kill are my two housemates, to secure the entire apartment for myself as my personal torture and killing chamber. After that, I will start luring people into my apartment, knock them out with a hammer, and slit their throats. I will torture some of the good-looking people before I kill them, assuming that the good-looking ones had the best sex lives."

"I will attack the very girls who represent everything I hate in the female gender: The hottest sorority of UCSB."

"The final solution to triumph over my enemies was to destroy them, to carry out my Day of Retribution, to exact my ultimate and devastating vengeance against all of the popular young people who never accepted me, and against all women for rejecting me and starving me of love and sex."

"How could an inferior, ugly black boy be able to get a white girl and not me? I am beautiful, and I am half white myself. I am descended from British aristocracy. He is descended from slaves. I deserve it more. I tried not to believe his foul words, but they were already said, and it was hard to erase from my mind. If this is actually true, if this ugly black filth was able to have sex with a blonde white girl at the age of thirteen while I've had to suffer virginity all my life, then this just proves how ridiculous the female gender is. They would give themselves to this filthy scum, but they reject ME? The injustice!"

"I didn't start this war. I wasn't the one who struck first. ... But I will finish it by striking back. I will punish everyone. And it will be beautiful. Finally, at long last, I can show the world my true worth."

Excellent stuff, isn't it? Rodger also details his plan to kill his stepmother and younger brother.

He did not carry that out, but he did fulfill some parts of his plan. I tried to read the whole thing myself but couldn't get through more than a few pages of it. I bailed. Oddly enough, his writing style wasn't terrible. It's a shame he became a certifiable lunatic. Within incel circles, Rodger became known as the "Supreme Gentleman Elliot Rodger." Suffice to say; this would inspire at least two more killings. In 2015, Chris Harper-Mercer shot nine and wounded eight others at Umpqua Community College in Roseburg, OR. He, too, killed himself, and he also left a manifesto. Alek Minassian drove a van into a group of people in Toronto, killing ten and hurting fourteen more. He was captured. He didn't have the decency to kill himself. He praised Eliot Rodger.

What can be done before the next killing occurs? It seems to me the best way is to enable incels so that they can have sex. I'm no Casanova, but I do have some experience in these matters. If not for the grace of reason and logic, maybe I might have become one of them myself though non-violent. These are simple suggestions, in no particular order:

- Stop being a loser. If you think of yourself as a loser, you are a loser. Gain confidence in yourself. Women find confidence very sexy. Just don't be obnoxious.

- Stop being a whiny cry-baby! There is nothing less attractive than someone who constantly bemoans his state in life. Grow a pair and face life head-on.

- Stop thinking women owe you anything! Human beings are autonomous. Women are not a country to be conquered or battle to be won. They are not property to be taken.

- Start thinking of women as humans like yourself. Women have the same desires and emotions you do. There are many female incels too, but they don't drive vans into crowds.

- Make friends with women. Get to know them as people. Learn their interests, their likes, and dislikes. If you get to know women, you might find you like them. A *possible* side benefit is they might sleep with you or introduce you to someone who will sleep with you. Don't expect it, but it might happen.

- Expand your interests. Actor Vincent Price once said, "The man who limits his interests, limits his life." This is true. Cultivating a variety of interests introduces you to new activities you can enjoy. It also makes you a more interesting person, which women find attractive as well as giving you a plethora of subjects to talk with them about.

- Stop looking to bed, "Stacys." It could happen, it has happened to me, but overall the attractive are going to gravitate to other beautiful people. That is the way of the world. Get over it. Learn to see the beauty of other women. Not every woman is or needs to be, a centerfold. Women have more to offer besides physical beauty, which eventually fades in any case. They have intelligence, kindness, caring, and generosity amongst their other traits. These are their essential traits. Remember the movie *Shallow Hal*? Hal only wanted to be with beautiful women. It was only after he saw the beauty in other women that he found happiness. Remember, you're probably no grand physical prize yourself.
- If you are not a physical prize yourself, do what you can to make yourself more attractive. Lose some weight, dress better, maybe even something simple like combing your hair. Women appreciate guys who take care of themselves. After all, you expect women to take care of themselves for *you*, why shouldn't you be expected to take care of yourself for *them*?

- If you do get a woman into bed, don't make everything about yourself. As I said, women have needs too. Use those first times as learning experiences. Learn to touch and be receptive to her touch. Prioritize her pleasure above your own. Make her the center of your world. You will find there is nothing more satisfying than having totally pleased a woman. She will do the same for you.

As another college friend used to say, "Virginity is curable." So, you incels need to set about curing your sickness. Either follow my suggestions or find your own way. Your current behavior is unacceptable. People shouldn't have to worry about some loser who can't get sex coming after them with a gun, van or whatever. If you don't fix yourselves, you only have two options. You can get that fistful of hundreds and head to the whorehouse, or you can kill yourself. Kill no one else, just yourself.

What About Our Children?

As you may have gathered from other chapters in this short treatise, I am a supporter of Eugenics. Because of our population problem, we can no longer afford for babies to be born haphazardly as they have been throughout human history. We have to be smarter than that now. Too long have we allowed the ignorant to reproduce and create children they don't have the intelligence, finances, psychological soundness, or sense of responsibility to raise correctly. These families usually wind up on welfare and/or Maury Povich. It is time to change that, and you know it.

Eugenics is about producing better human beings. The word means "well-born." Whether we do it via DNA manipulation or old-fashioned breeding techniques, it is an idea whose time has come back. In the old days, eugenic breeding choices were unfortunately motivated by racism or some other ridiculous reasoning. Current objections to eugenics include fear of reproduction being restricted based on what political group is in control. These difficulties can be prevented by having computers make determinations. Today, we can perfect the selection of positive traits scientifically through standardized tests and information gathering.

Anyone who wishes to become pregnant, or has already become pregnant, must come to government offices for a license. You cannot have a child without a permit. Why not? You cannot drive a car or boat without a license. Nor can you practice law or medicine. It seems that having children should be at least as important as these things are. Grants will be permitted depending on the current birth rate and the results of the testing. Abortion will be free and legal for those who do not want children. The parents, yes, there should be two. It is too difficult for one person to raise a child by themselves; understanding sometimes it cannot be avoided, such as in the case of the death of one parent. Be they either man/woman, man/man or woman/woman they must provide complete heath and family records as well as financial information. They must also submit to a comprehensive psychological examination. This exam will help determine their sense of responsibility and emotional health. This procedure should, for the most part, prevent both bad parenting and actual child abuse.

Next, the pregnancy must be monitored. Most of this will simply be by regular visits to their doctor as it is done now. Occasionally (perhaps once a trimester), appointments will be paid to the home. It is to ensure the parents have everything they need to have a healthy baby as well as determine whether or not the pregnancy should be terminated if things are not going well or conditions are unsuitable.

When the baby is born (only one child at a time with a maximum of two excluding twins, triplets and so on) the mother will be given at least twelve weeks maternity leave to allow mother and child to bond, perhaps one or two weeks for the other partner as well. All costs for pregnancy and birth will be paid for by the government.

At a time specified by professionals, testing will begin. The first testing will be the same as it is today. Making sure the baby is healthy and progressing at the normal levels.

When the child begins school, he/she will be tested to see if they are sociable and have good psychological health. Their intelligence level will also be checked. These tests will also be conducted every few years. If there are problems, the child can be worked with in any of the areas the child needs help. As high school graduation approaches, they will be given yet another test. If the child cannot pass the exams, and this cannot be rectified through more intense instruction, he/she will be put to death. This option will be available throughout their education if they become uncontrollable. Over the years, students seem to be disrespecting their teachers increasingly. I saw a video recently that showed a teacher disrespected and physically threatened by students who had the nerve to stream it online. If I had been their parents, I would have killed them myself.

I know this sounds harsh, but it is not. It will prevent those who cannot handle life spared having to live it. If they are not intelligent, they will not have to have jobs they will neither like nor can do. If they have violent or criminal tendencies, they will be spared the guilt of hurting people. Their parents will also be saved the pain of their children being criminals.

There will be one more group of tests upon finishing college and/or trade school if they decide to go. Once they pass this series of tests, which are the same ones they have had all their lives, they are done and ready to assume the honor and responsibility of being an adult.

We must stop treating childbearing and rearing like, as a friend of mine noted, a cottage industry. If children are essential to the human race, we should treat them with the importance they deserve.

Educational Crisis

We have an education crisis in this country. It is not because we have bad teachers who don't care. We do have good teachers. Many teachers spend their own money on supplies and give much of their own time to educate their students. The problem is we have allowed our educational system to become a political football. Republicans and their Owners, who think people should only be educated enough to run the machines and do the paperwork, want to cut education and, in some cases, want to get rid of colleges completely except to serve as further vocational training. Add to that the god-worshippers, who wish to use the schools as indoctrination for their cults. Students have incredible obstacles to learning.

Look at Republicans. They have long sought to end education funding either by cutting it directly or by diverting to private or religious schools. This way, private schools make more profit. One of the Republican goals is to privatize all schools, so only those who can pay for it will get a real education. Of course, that education will be controlled by the Owners. No more philosophy, women or ethnic studies, the study of the great American novel, or anything else that is not focused on business and/or the running of factories. Republicans (and many Democrats) want a Corporate States of

America. Money is their god. Speaking of gods, this leads us to-

God-worshippers. In this country, it is the Christian cult with which we mainly have to deal. However, wherever god-worshippers are hatred, treason, murder, and other terrible things follow. Like Republicans, the cults want to destroy public education. Many Christians are also Republicans. The goals are quite similar; keep people ignorant while adding the desire to indoctrinate children into the Christian cult. When people are uninformed, they are easily controlled. Add to that the authority of the "Creator of the Universe," and you have dictatorial gold. With this, god-worshippers can push anti-science like creationism. They want people to be stupid like they are.

Now we have Betsy DeVos. She is the fulfillment of Republicans' and religionists' wildest masturbatory fantasies. Like other Trump appointees, she seeks to destroy the very department she now heads. She aims to destroy education itself and replace it with indoctrination to the Christian cult. DeVos is a billionaire from a billionaire family. She bought the Cabinet position by donating to Republicans and Donald Trump, whom she once referred to as an "interloper" in the Republican Party.

DeVos explained her philosophy in the September 6, 1997 edition of *Roll Call,* a newspaper that covers the United States Congress:

"I have decided, however, to stop taking offense at the suggestion that we are buying influence. Now I simply concede the point. They are right. We do expect some things in return.
We expect to foster a conservative governing philosophy consisting of limited government and respect for traditional American virtues. We expect a return on our investment; we expect a good and honest government. Furthermore, we expect the Republican Party to use the money to promote these policies, and yes, to win elections."

DeVos' preferred method is to get people to want vouchers (also the Republican strategy) to take away funding from public schools, further limiting their effectiveness. Parents who use these schools say they should get vouchers to compensate them for paying for public schools. What they forget, or conveniently ignore, is the people who do not or ever had children in school. They pay school tax too. So, where are their checks or tax credits? You pay school tax not just to send your children to school but to send everyone's children to school. Why? Because an educated populace is beneficial to everyone.

How do we fix this? As with everything else, we must overthrow the system that created the situation and allows it to continue. We need to follow the Christian strategy and take over every school district in the country or get a president who will issue executive orders. Common Core does not go far enough. We need a national curriculum for all schools. No one can opt-out. We need national education standards, so colleges, businesses, and the military will know people have met specific criteria for knowledge. Top priorities should include science. Hard science, as seen by scientists. To quote the late Carl Sagan, "Children are natural scientists." Scientific ideas could be introduced as early as kindergarten. In the first grade, they should also start learning critical thinking skills. These skills will teach children *how* to think, not *what* to think. This idea has long been opposed by both Republicans (probably some Democrats as well) and god-worshippers. They don't want children to be intelligent. Again, it is so they can be controlled. Students must be exposed to everything: books, art, music, political ideologies, and civics. Anything and everything must be taught. Schools must also include life skills like sex education, home economics, woodshop, gardening, and other "adulting" skills to prepare them for life.

Furthermore, teachers must be paid a decent salary so that they can work towards this goal. Educators often must get second jobs just to make ends meet. That is why you see more strikes by teachers across the country. If your child's education is as important as you say it is, your kid's teacher should not also be your cashier at the local Walmart.

Students need to be tested at least once every few years to ensure they are growing intellectually, emotionally, and socially. If they are struggling, they must be helped. If they are merely lazy, making a conscious decision not to learn or become a criminal, they must be removed. We can no longer afford people who drag society down. The United States once had one of the best educational systems in the world. We can make it again.

Science: Our Only Oracle

Science

('saɪəns)

n

1. the systematic study of the nature and behavior of the material and physical universe, based on observation, experiment, and measurement, and the formulation of laws to describe these facts in general terms
2. the knowledge so obtained or the practice of obtaining it
3. any particular branch of this knowledge: *the pure and applied sciences*.
4. any body of knowledge organized in a systematic manner
5. skill or technique
6. *archaic* knowledge
[C14: via Old French from Latin *Scientia* knowledge, from *scīre* to know]

Collins English Dictionary – Complete and Unabridged, 12th Edition 2014 © HarperCollins Publishers 1991, 1994, 1998, 2000, 2003, 2006, 2007, 2009, 2011, 2014

Science knows what we know. It is also the method of how we know what we know. Science is our purest form of truth. From the earliest beginnings of civilization, we have been curious about how our world works.

For instance, an experiment attributed to Eratosthenes of Cyrene, a Greek mathematician and head of the Library of Alexandria, demonstrated he was not only a proponent of a spherical Earth (which the Greeks had suggested even earlier), but you could also know how big it is. Eratosthenes was aware an obelisk in Alexandria cast no shadow at noon while a pillar in another city did cast a shadow at the same time. He reasoned this would only be possible on a round Earth. Then Eratosthenes hired a man to pace out the distance between the two obelisks. From that, he could determine the size of the earth to high precision. He only had an error of a few percent. Thank you, Carl Sagan, *Cosmos,* and NASA!

Science makes discoveries and proves facts through a process known as the *scientific method.* The method is a series of steps:

1. Observation and description of a phenomenon or group of events.

2. Formulation of a hypothesis to explain the phenomena. In physics, the assumption often takes the form of a causal mechanism or a mathematical relation.

3. Use of the explanation to predict the existence of other phenomena, or to predict the results of new observations quantitatively.

4. Performance of experimental tests of the predictions by several independent experimenters and correctly performed experiments.

Source: rochester.edu

This manner is the way all human problems should be approached. Science works so well because it employs logic and reason. These are things most humans do not use well, if at all. In any case, science has created a safer, more comfortable life for those of us lucky enough to live in the first world countries. We need to extend the influence of science to the entire world. While we are at it, we also need to spread that influence in this country too. More and more, science is being attacked.

Believe it or not, some do not believe in science. These people resist, hate, and fear science. They loathe it because they do not understand it, or it undermines their superstitions. They seek to legislate science, and unfortunately, they have the ear of many politicians, who also have the goal of keeping people ignorant. For the most part, these people are god-worshippers. While it is true some religious people are and have been great scientists, in modern times, it is because they compartmentalize their lives. An interesting factoid: 93% of those in the National Academy of Sciences are professed Atheists, with a similar number in the UK's Royal Academy of Sciences.

Science deniers are made up of three groups of people: shills who do their denying on behalf of some corporate entity. These are the ones who speak against climate change or deny that smoking causes cancer. The second group is New Age idiots complaining about vaccines, homeopathic medicine advocates, or those who push "spiritual" nonsense. The largest group being the previously mentioned religionists. They are the most threatening group as well. They hate science mainly, but not exclusively, because of the theory of evolution. You no doubt have heard the expression, "It's only a theory." This comment demonstrates how ignorant these people are. Scientific theories are much different from the word theory as it is used in the common vernacular. To most people, a theory is "Colonel Mustard did it in the library with the pipe wrench." That is what would be more correctly referred to as a hypothesis. A scientific theory is described in this way:

"A **scientific theory** is a well-substantiated explanation of some aspect of the natural world that is acquired through the scientific method and repeatedly tested and confirmed, preferably using a written, pre-defined protocol of observations and experiments. Scientific theories are the most reliable, rigorous, and comprehensive form of scientific knowledge."

 Source: Schafersman, Steven D. *"An Introduction to Science"*; quoted by Wikipedia

The point is, a scientific hypothesis must be tested and retested before it earns the status of theory. You don't think the "scientists" over at the Creation Museum do that, do you? They just make stuff up out of whole cloth to bring things in line with their superstitious belief system.

Another high point about science is it is self-correcting. If something in science is incorrect, scientists will discover the error and correct it. An amateur archaeologist named Charles Dawson claimed he had fossils from a previously unknown biological ancestor. For over forty years, the find was considered a controversial but significant piece in the study of human evolution. In 1953, it was confirmed Piltdown Man was indeed a forgery. It was a combination of a human skull, the lower jawbone of an orangutan, and teeth from a chimpanzee that had been stained with an iron solution. It was science that found the forgery. Science had corrected itself.

Have you ever heard of a religion correcting itself? No, and you won't either. Part of the attraction of faith is the concept it will never change. You only need to learn something once, and that's it. Science is always evolving and revising itself. The more we learn, the more their god gets pushed into the corner of irrelevance. That is what frightens them. The story cannot change, or it casts doubt on everything they believe. Uncertainty is the killer of religions.

An excellent example of this fear of science is Dayton, Tennessee. This town is where the Scopes Trial was held. On the defense was science teacher and football coach John Scopes. He was accused of teaching evolution (the favorite fundamentalist target) in the high school in violation of Tennessee's Butler Act. It was the theory of evolution that was on trial and, to the greater extent, science itself. During the famous eight-day trial, the case was argued by two legal giants; three-time presidential candidate William Jennings Bryan and legendary lawyer Clarence Darrow. When the judge, John T. Raulston, forbade the experts Darrow had brought in to explain evolution to the jury (who were not even in the courtroom most of the time), Darrow had to come up with a new strategy. He did. Darrow called prosecuting attorney William Jennings Bryan to the stand! He would testify as an authority on the Bible. Despite his own team's protests, Bryan wanted to do it. Darrow deposed him asking classic village Atheist questions. He got Bryan to admit under oath that the six days of creation in Genesis could have been millions of years. Bryan still won the case. Scopes was convicted (later overturned), but Bryan lost the war. Dayton, which only arrested Scopes in the first place to garner publicity for their town with the trial, became the laughing stock of the country. Bryan himself died a few days later. Scopes could not remember if he taught evolution or not. In any case, he was using the *standard* biology text for the state of Tennessee; *A Civic Biology: Presented in Problems* (New York, 1914) by George William Hunter.

The point to this short trip through history is that every year Dayton hosts a festival celebrating the Scopes trial. I attended the festival one year with my friends from the Atlanta Freethought Society. There is now a statue of Bryan and, more recently, Darrow as well (although one Christian woman said she was going to shoot it) classic cars and a sign to "Read Your Bible" sponsored by Coca-Cola, supposedly to be historically accurate. There was such a sign in 1925, but I don't remember it having corporate sponsorship. The most exciting event of the festival is a play based on the trial. It is very accurate. This play is unique since it is produced and performed by members of Bryan College, founded by funds Bryan left to the town. When I was there, before the play started, locals sang such fun songs of the period as "You Can't Make A Monkey Out of Me" with one of the singers pointing at me. We did have a fun day, and I think they enjoyed having us. After all, how often do they get real Atheists there? It was apparent; however, nothing had really changed at all. They still look upon evolution and probably science in general with fear, suspicion, and superstition. This fear is the burden we must overcome.

Overcoming this burden will be even more difficult now. President Trump appointed, and Congress approved Congressman Jim Bridenstine (R-OK) as head of NASA. NASA is the premier scientific agency of the United States. It was NASA that took us to the moon, and other planets, that sent human-made objects to travel into interstellar space. Bridenstine was a known climate change denier, although he has changed his viewpoint. He still has never run a large government agency before and is not a scientist.

Other items suggest he will not be a good fit. He is focused on space exploration but not pure science, which provides the knowledge to do space exploration. He seems to be another Trump lackey. If Bridenstine is like Trump's other associates, he could work to tear down the agency or try to convert it to purely commercial goals.

Science is the way we have found to the modern world. It is the science that should be the primary method to run our lives. Should we believe mythology and lies? No! There was a time when human beings were guided by stories and what little we could discern about the natural world. As time went on, we became more curious and wanted to learn how the world worked. It was at this point science was born. Through the centuries, we did exactly that. Now, we are at the point where we have learned as much knowledge in the last fifty years as we had in all of human history. We were able to do this because science searches for truth. Truth must be our guide. As Neil deGrasse Tyson likes to say: "The good thing about science is that it is true whether or not you believe in it."

True or False?

You hear about it every day on the news. Can you trust the news? You are barraged with information from various news outlets, but which one can you trust? There seem to be a million news sources; newspapers and magazines, radio and television, and the Internet. The Internet, the most significant source of information and misinformation the world has ever known.

Can you trust the news? Is it true and accurate? Well, yes and no. Yes, in a sense, legitimate news organizations strive to report the news accurately. They do fact-check. Donald Trump does not understand this because the former reality star has his own reality, and facts rarely come into his world. The same goes for the ministers of propaganda Kellyanne Conway, Sean Spicer (now gone), and Sarah Huckabee Sanders, who mostly just parrot whatever their master says. No, in a sense, the media often under reports stories based on the interests of their Owners. For instance, you rarely saw reports on the Dakota Pipeline conflict, and during the 2016 campaign, you rarely heard about Bernie Sanders until he got so big they could no longer afford to ignore him. Why is that? Because the Owners own the media. Many of the Owners have interests in the subjects the news is reporting on. The large corporations also wanted their puppet Hillary Clinton to win. You cannot fully trust the media. You cannot even trust the book you are reading right now unless you check and confirms what it is saying.

Flashback to fifty or sixty years ago, the news was purer. The media was not entirely owned by multinational corporations. It is correct several newspapers might be held by a news corporation, some of them might own local radio and television stations, but their focus was news. For the pre-cable television and radio networks, the news divisions were sources of pride. While not perfect, there was a commitment to being truthful and accurate. Sometimes there would be mistakes; sometimes, a false or misleading story would be printed or broadcast. Often these would be deliberate. Perhaps to help capture a criminal or to protect secrets, and would be corrected afterward. Overall, you could more or less trust what you were reading/watching/listening. These were the days of Edward R. Murrow and Walter Cronkite.

Those days are gone. News has been corrupted. What has caused this? Several things. First, large corporations now own and therefore control the major news outlets while adding some of their own. CNN and Time magazine are owned by Time-Warner. Fox News is owned by the Fox Entertainment Group, which is in turn owned by

Rupert Murdoch. MSNBC is owned by Comcast, ABC is owned by Disney, and so on. Because of this, the news now reflects the views of their owners. It is alright for news programs to promote a particular viewpoint, but it must be labeled as such. In newspapers, they still do this in the op-ed columns. On television, they no longer do this. In the old days, the word "commentary" would appear on the screen whenever opinions were given. Now we have whole television programs, such as the (now gone) *O'Reilly Factor*, that are nothing but opinion. Uncritical viewers will assume this is the news, like Walter Cronkite was, and will blindly believe it. Since Ronald Reagan scrapped the Fairness Doctrine in 1987 (the FCC rule that required broadcast media to provide time for discussion of all sides of controversial issues), suppression of other viewpoints is now standard practice. We need to bring back the Fairness Doctrine.

Yet another problem is how Americans view the news nowadays. News is now considered a form of entertainment. "Infotainment" I've heard it called. News should be like getting gas or picking up milk at the store. It is something you need. Stop, get the story, and leave. There is no reason to spend hours reading or watching the news unless for watching election results or if you're writing a book. Yes, you might be a news junkie and want to know everything about a particular issue, and that's ok, but don't spend all your time with the news.

There is now a further obstacle to receiving honest news: Sinclair Broadcast Group, another organ for conservative views. Unlike Fox, their business model consists of buying up local television stations. This idea is smart because Sinclair can now trade on the excellent reputations these stations have built up over the years to push their agenda. How many people would know that the TV station they have been watching for years (perhaps decades) is now owned by a company that wants to influence their political views?

Let's move on to the Internet. The main problem with the Internet is practically anyone can set up or, worse, impersonate a news site. While you can trust some of them to be real, you must first check them out, see if they line up with other news sources and see if they are consistent. Even if they are authentic, more likely than not, they will be pushing a viewpoint. I like The Young Turks, Buzzfeed, and Ring of Fire, but I have no illusions about them being anything but left-leaning sites. I read the Daily Caller and Breitbart sometimes as well, even though I find Breitbart increasingly annoying. For unbiased information, try ontheissues.org, WikiLeaks, and Wikipedia as well. Much of the fake news comes from people just flat out making things up to create "clickbait." Stories to entice the lesser-educated by reinforcing their prejudices. They make money at this and feel no obligation to fact check or be truthful. I used to trust Politifact but have cooled on them since they claimed that Hillary Clinton was the most honest candidate. There are other fact-checking sites, try Snopes.com.

Ok, now we see the problem. What's the solution? It is twofold: heavy regulation and people taking responsibility for the information that comes to them. Please understand which I am talking. I do not want to interfere with the freedom of the press. I want to make the news truthful. I think what we need is an oversight organization, paid for by public money but independent, that will fact check every story that comes from all media. All news could be funneled here first then released to the public after it is determined to be true. Another way would be to allow the release of the report first then confirm the accuracy of the story. If the account is found to be inaccurate, the media outlet would have to pay a considerable fine in addition to total retraction and apologies. The problem I see with this second method is false information will get out there, and it is human nature to believe the first thing they hear. This rule will mainly apply to radio/TV/Internet since newspapers and magazines have a more extended period to confirm information. However, if their work is also inaccurate, the same fines would be imposed. Furthermore, these conditions would only concern unintentional misinformation. For intentional disinformation, there will be a harsher penalty, the same as I propose for the Internet.

The Internet. Most would say it cannot and should not be regulated. I agree for the most part. However, there must be some rules. The unscrupulous, driven by either greed or darker purposes, seek to spread false information. We have seen this with the Russian practice of planting fake stories to manipulate the American people. For society to function correctly, it must depend on all information to be true and accurate. Fake news sites and others that push hokum, illogic, and false data must be stopped. Some of these sites which spread relatively harmless dreck may be punished by fines. The more severe offenders that seek to influence politics and law must be dealt with more severely. Since the world could turn on the false information they provide, I suggest the penalty should be death for those responsible. It is the same penalty I propose for all media that deliberately spreads such falsehoods. After a period of punishment, the rest of the potential liars will get the message. The result will be the news you can trust.

Don't Take Anything on Faith

I watched a college-sponsored debate on the existence of "God" the other day. The link was sent to me by a friend who was one of the participants in the discussion. The debate question was, "Does God Exist?" It was sponsored, as these things usually are, by the campus religionist group, which, as these things are generally, Christian. The other sponsor was the campus Atheist/Humanist group. I find these confrontations informative and entertaining, so anxiously watched it.

It was an exciting exchange. It was because the debate attempted to address the question on a more scholarly level than any other discussion I had heard before. The positive argument was taken by a professional philosopher who teaches at the university. I imagine he is Christian, but he argued for the "classical theism" proposed by Aristotle and Aquinas. It was a unique strategy. Perhaps he thought if he could get you to believe in a classical interpretation of God or at least, gods in general, you would later come to believe in his god-thing.

My friend, who is not a philosopher (his doctorate is in education), wasn't buying any of it. He pointed out all his opponent's arguments were based on his starting with his conclusion first. That is, there is a god. From that, he seeks to find evidence to support this conclusion. This approach is the mistake every religionist makes. Maybe this is the only way they can debate the question even if they do realize they are arguing from a house built on sand. As my friend noted, he did not prove his case.

I did enjoy the debate. It was refreshing to hear a discussion on a more intellectual level instead of the usual highly illogical, emotional knuckle-dragging Evangelical/Fundamentalist point of view. Still, those simpler debates do tend to address the real crux of the argument which this debate did not as much; does God exist? That's the real question, really the only issue. Something either exists or does not exist. It is either real or not. The answer to any reasonable person would be no. You can try to bury everything in a pile of philosophical excrement, but it doesn't work. When you say there is a god (or anything else), you are making a physical statement about the world. Therefore, you must produce proof, empirical evidence that supports your position. If I told you little green men landed in my yard last night, you would be a fool if you did not ask me for proof.

Religious people seldom (if ever) ask for proof. If you tell them something that reinforces their beliefs or prejudices, they suspend all skepticism. That is the great danger of religion. It teaches people not to think. Religionists think this is a good thing. Those who do not think do not question. They can be led down any path the religious leader wants.

As quoted earlier, but worth repeating, Voltaire stated: "Those who can make you believe absurdities can make you commit atrocities." Was he ever right! The ship of religion sails upon an ocean of blood. Humans have been killing for their gods since the dawn of humankind. Human sacrifice is stock and trade for god-worshipers even now. Look at the Middle East. Although there is now a political component to their fanaticism, it is still the old "My god can kill your god…" they have been spouting for millennia. Even in the United States, we see this same insanity. I'm not just talking about 9/11. We have had witch burnings, persecution of other religious sects, and outright terrorist acts like Robert L. Dear Jr, the shooter at the Planned Parenthood in 2015 or Anitra Braxton, who in December 2015 shot her friend in the eye for not believing in her god and then kept the body on her couch as a "shrine to God." That's just two incidents from 2015.

I'm sure some of you are thinking, "Don't Atheists commit murder too?" Yes, there was an Atheist who did a murder, just one. On February 10, 2015, Craig Stephen Hicks murdered three innocent Muslims in Chapel Hill, North Carolina. He did not kill them "in the name of Atheism." No one ever has been. He murdered these people over a parking space. He may have been an Atheist, but he certainly was not a rational one.

Interestingly, it was reported by the national press (until Hicks' website/homepage was taken down) he had supported Muslims, gay rights and respected others' beliefs. It was not a hate crime, per se. This guy just snapped. Unfortunately, he had guns. However, at least some sanity returned, and he turned himself into the police that same evening. The Humanist/Atheist community was devastated. It is not the sort of thing we are used to, as opposed to religious communities like Christians and Muslims, where this is business as usual. In typical politically correct fashion, there was a push to label this a hate crime.

You see, the incident was so jarring because non-believers are such peaceful people. We abhor violence and killing. Unfortunately, this makes us doormats to the murderous god-worshippers. They have been taught and trained from birth to hate, or at least distrust anyone outside of their cult. This behavior is because, to use the anthropological term, religions are tribal. Religious believers want to kill us, they always have. So, what are we going to do about it?

It is not like the non-religious have done nothing. Atheist and Humanist Groups like American Atheists, Freedom from Religion Foundation, Center for Inquiry, American Humanist Association, Secular Coalition for America, and others have fought the good fight. The problem is what we have done has not been as effective as it should have been. We have defended the First Amendment voraciously. For those who may not recall the specific language, it reads thus:

"Congress shall make no law respecting an establishment of religion, or prohibiting the free exercise thereof, or abridging the freedom of speech, or the press, or the right of the people peacefully to assemble, and to petition the Government for a redress of grievances."

-- The First Amendment to the United States Constitution

Ennobling words. Words you think any American would be proud of and be willing to give their lives for, and they do, to a large extent. However, there is one segment of society who do not feel that way, the religious. Indeed, not all of them. There are people like Barry Lynn, a minister who ran the civil rights group Americans United for Separation of Church and State, which champions the rights of all Americans.

Unfortunately, they are in the minority. A Public Policy Polling survey conducted in February 2015 found 57% of Republicans want to remove the establishment clause and make Christianity the official religion of the United States. This group includes those in political office and even their candidates for president like Rick Perry, Mike Huckabee, and Ben Carson. We are seeing this now with President Donald Trump. Trump knows religious people are stupid and easily led. Keeping people ignorant is a big part of the political goal. Why do you think Betsy DeVos was made Secretary of Education? The survey also found 2/3 of Republicans do not accept climate change, and 49% do not accept evolution. This data melds perfectly with the beliefs of Dominionists, who support a complete takeover of society, including the government. More about them later.

As for Democrats, overall, they seem to support church/state separation, but they still kowtow to religionists. WARNING: PERSONAL ANECDOTE: I went to one of former New Jersey governor Jon Corzine's town meetings. After his talk, there was time for a short question and answer period, but I was not called on. Corzine had to leave, so I didn't get to ask my question about taxing churches. He wasn't getting away from me that easily. I walked right up to the stage and asked him why we don't tax churches. He replied, "We can't do that!" He had the sound of disdain in his voice. Why can't we? Why do religions hold special privileges in society? They do nothing to earn it. They just con people into thinking they earn it by occasionally doing some charitable work, so people think they should not pay taxes. This attitude is a violation of the Constitution. There is a separation of church and state, but that does not give churches the right to dodge taxes and not be good neighbors.

As we see now, the Democratic Party is becoming more conservative thanks to the repulsive influence of the Clintons. This change is because Democrats have become all about the money mainly. After all, the Clintons are all about the money. The Democrats ignored their progressive base in the hopes of securing large sums of corporate money. They thought Hillary Clinton could bring in that money, which is why they supported her. Next, Democrats will be looking at religionists, particularly Evangelicals, to satisfy their dreams of avarice. They have seen how easily Evangelicals, and religionists in general, can be manipulated by a Donald Trump and they want their share. Politicians have always known religious people tend to be of low intelligence. Therefore, Donald Trump loves the poorly educated.

It now brings us to the Dominionists. If you don't know about them, you should. Also referred to as Christian Reconstructionism, they are one of, if not the, most treasonous of all the Christian sects. They advocate the literal takeover of American society. From the government to entertainment, they seek the *domination* of everything. All cults seek to control those within their sphere.

Furthermore, they hate America, they always have. Almost all religionists hate America. Their loyalty is to their god, their prophet, their savior. Even if they might seem to be reasonable, it only takes the right (I hate this word) trigger to set god-worshippers off into violence. Suddenly, that quiet, respectful lad you live next door to has become a gun-toting lunatic.

Imagine the kind of world Dominionists will create. All laws will be based on Biblical law. Anyone who wants an abortion or a divorce, is homosexual, who simply is not Christian, will be persecuted, and punished, possibly with death. There will be prescribed methods of behavior, and dissent is forbidden. Since religion is tribal, expect the purging of undesirables, which is everybody but them. Expect a church tax, segregation, perhaps even a return of slavery. Remember, slaveholders forced Christianity onto the slaves to instill the belief they were meant to be slaves. This tactic was so effective that it is only now, almost 160 years after slavery ended, that African-Americans non-believers are coming into their own. They are addressing the stigma the cult has placed upon them. Cultists believe anyone, not of the cult, is an enemy, a sub-human. Therefore, it is not a big deal to enslave those they perceive as inferiors.

Recently, a new wrinkle was added. A new Christian movement called Independent Network Charismatic. A new name, same old goal; take over and destroy the United States of America. Religionists will not quit. They must be stopped.

Let us not forget the other, possibly even more bloodthirsty cult, Islam, although most Muslims are undoubtedly peaceful. Muslims have not had the benefit of a Renaissance and secularization to help modify or negate their beliefs. Beliefs most Americans and other Westerners would agree are extreme are commonplace. Death for apostasy, the subjugation of women, death for homosexuals, et al., are pretty much mainstream positions for Muslims despite what they may say publicly. Sam Harris provides a video on his website that is instructive. The link is on Sam Harris' website: samharris.org. Islam is no religion of peace. What religion is?

Therefore, they must be stopped—all of them. I know what you are going to ask: "Don't many churches do good things? Don't they help the poor?" Some do, but that is not a reason to continue their existence. Secular organizations do the same things without the danger that they will attempt to influence those they help to join a cult. That is the real reason religions help people at all. They wish to glorify their god-thing but also, and mainly, to expand the cult. Your next (or other) question will be: "Don't people have a right to believe in a god?" No, they do not. They have a legal right but not an ethical right. You do not have a right to believe anything for which you cannot provide empirical evidence. Just as important, you do not have a right to try to convince others to believe in anything where there is no empirical evidence. Religion is a con job.

Any good con artist knows they must get their victim (the mark) to be a willing participant in actions that will ultimately be harmful to them. The problem is this con game, due to the centuries of propagation, has become reciprocal. In the past, the church used the state, or the state used the church to rule. This reality prompted the well-known quote by Seneca the Younger: "Religion is regarded by the common people as true, by the wise as false, and by the rulers as useful." Now, at least in the United States, our politicians believe religious nonsense and the churches believe in the power of politics. There may be politicians and churches who don't subscribe to this way of thinking, but they are not the ones controlling your lives, are they?

Atheists, Humanists, and other non-believers must change society. We must no longer be doormats for the religionists. We must be willing to fight and take the battle to them. I know it is against our nature, but we must get guns and learn how to use them. We must encourage Atheist scientists and entrepreneurs to create new and powerful technologies, including weapons of war, for our use exclusively. We must stop depending on the First Amendment to fight our battles for us because it might soon be repealed. We have a Republican-controlled Congress, Senate, and White House with a manipulative (and easily manipulated) idiot for president. Perhaps we could get one of us to bend Trump's ear? Possibly one of us could be his Iago? An Iago with a noble purpose? I doubt it. Trump listens to the god-worshipers or at least pretends to. He nominated anti-education religionist Betsy DeVos to be Secretary of Education. This appointment, along with Creationist Vice President Mike Pence, demonstrates Trump is more than willing to give religionists their way so long as it does not interfere with business. Trump does this because he is ignorant of the matter, not realizing good education is necessary for business. Maybe he just doesn't care.

What people must learn is religion is not their friend; it is their enslaver. I've met too many Atheists desperate to believe in "religious liberty" so much they are willing to concede the rights of Atheists to maintain an uneasy and illogical peace. There are too many religionists (in this country, Christian) who think they have many privileges, and it gives them the right to do anything they want to do, including killing. Don't believe me? Just read the hate mail every Atheist/Humanist organization receives.

An interesting side note: In China, religion has come back with a vengeance in the post-Mao era. China has had religions spring up again for years now. Even the flagship Christian sect has had a presence in China for years. There is the state-sanctioned Catholic church and many unauthorized by both China and the Vatican. Now, the Catholic church is working with the Communist government over a sticking point of selecting bishops. The Catholics want to create a strong foothold in China because they see many potential cultists (not to mention all the young boys they can molest) in that country. Right now, in China, Buddhism is the most popular religion at 185-250 million, with Christianity coming in second with 72-92 million. This information was reported by James Griffiths and Matt Rivers of CNN in an article dated February 28, 2017. Lately, however, it seems the bloom is off that rose. China is once again cracking down on the Christian cult.

I was once an advocate for the First Amendment, for the separation of church and state. What I have seen in my nearly sixty years has made me an advocate for the church being destroyed by the state. Naturally, this brings up the specter of communism, which has always opposed the churches. The USSR and China failed because it only wanted to replace the dictatorship of the church with the tyranny of communism. They never wanted to free the people's minds truly. I would have been perfectly content to allow religion to die a natural death as humans became more intelligent. Unfortunately, it was not to be. With the election of Donald Trump, the religionists have gotten bolder. They feel it is within their grasp to take over the country and force their Bronze/Iron Age superstitions on all of us. We must fight or die.

The die is cast; we must revise this country's way of thinking. Religion must be made illegal, and those who promote it must be prosecuted, up to and including death for those who promote violence. If all the suggestions in this book are followed, this will happen naturally. Religionists want to enslave or kill us; do not doubt that. Religion has been responsible for many, if not most, of the wars and movements of suppression, such as the Witch Trials and the Crusades. Faith has held our scientific, social, and ethical evolution back for centuries. We will replace their destructive god belief with freedom.

Is It Time?

In modern-day Germany, the swastika is banned. So are other symbols of Nazism, such as Nazi salutes and *Mein Kampf.* While I disagree with banning books, any book, I can understand why Germany would do so. Nazism devastated Germany. The country that had given the world giants like Johannes Gutenberg, Johannes Kepler, and Ludwig van Beethoven had also spawned Adolph Hitler, Heinrich Himmler, and Joseph Goebbels. Some think this approach is repressive and may not be valid. We'll come back to that later.

Back in 2015, there was much discussion about removing Confederate symbols, such as statues, from society. Once again, this is understandable. While we must always acknowledge our past atrocities, I do not see the need to allow the symbols of those atrocities to confront us every day. Yes, memorials honoring the victims of these horrors are appropriate but not those that glorify them.

If something is harmful or destructive to society, society has the right and obligation to ban it. We routinely have criminalized activities that are detrimental to society, such as murder, rape, theft, drug abuse, and so on. However, we have yet to outlaw the most dangerous practice of all. We celebrate it. We let it into our homes. We allow it into our politics and civic life. We do this despite the misery, hate, and bloodshed for which it is responsible. This thing is religion—perhaps the most destructive force in history.

Religion has always been destructive. I have no doubt prehistoric tribes fought over whatever gods they believed in. Those who believe in gods love to kill. Maybe it is because of a fear of the god, perhaps because it gave them an excuse to kill. In any case, they die. Somewhere along the way, they came up with the charming idea of sacrifice, the motivation to give a life (someone or something else's of course) to the god for its approval and blessing. Sometimes this would be accomplished by the simple slitting of the throat, sometimes with an elaborate ritual and the extraction of the heart as the Aztecs did.

In the Bible, most know the story of Abraham. It is from Abraham we get the term Abrahamic religions, referring to Judaism, Christianity, and Islam. In the story, God commands Abraham to sacrifice his son Isaac to him as a burnt offering (apparently God loves the smell of burning flesh.)

"Take your son, your only son – yes, Isaac, whom you love so much – and go to the land of Moriah. Sacrifice him there as a burnt offering on one of the mountains, which I will point out to you." (Genesis 22:1-18)

Any parent in their right mind would react to this with pure horror, but Abraham was a religious man. He dutifully takes poor Isaac to the mountains and builds an altar. Abraham even has his son Isaac help him, having lied to Isaac about their purpose. Then he laid Isaac down on the altar and was about to kill him when God lets him off the hook. It was just a test of his faith! What's the matter, Abe, can't you take a joke? God was still in the mood for some barbeque, so he has Abraham burn a ram instead.

Eventually, these religions would keep their sacrifices to animals, although human sacrifice continued in Mesoamerica and continues in some countries in Africa today. However, religions kill not only for blessings; they kill to exterminate enemies and to control. In the year 415 CE, Hypatia of Alexandria, teacher, mathematician, and philosopher was murdered by Christians. They didn't just strangle and stone her, as portrayed in the film

Agora. They killed her by flaying the flesh from her with either shells or potshards. Her limbs were then burned. Her murder was instigated by the Bishop of Alexandria, Cyril. After her death, the vestiges of learning that had once made Alexandrea one of the great centers of ancient civilization were destroyed. Cyril was later made a saint.

After Rome fell, darkness fell on Europe as well. This period is generally referred to as the Dark Ages. It is the time when classical knowledge was largely forgotten, and the Christian cult held sway. It was a time of fear, fear of God, fear of Satan, fear of magic, fear of the unknown. What little learning there was took place in monasteries, which not only controlled the peasants' spiritual lives but also owned much of the land and wealth as well. It was also in this timeframe (approximately the 7th Century) that Islam was founded. Islam expanded itself through the use of the sword. Islam was no religion of peace as the world would discover. Meanwhile, back in Europe, the medieval period lasted for approximately one thousand years until the Renaissance began in the 14th Century.

The Renaissance was one of the great moments in human history. Much of the ancient knowledge was reclaimed. Ironically, much of this recovering was done by Islamic scholars during what is referred to as the Islamic Golden Age. In the west, religion's influence was diminished. The world began to learn again. This learning led to the Age of Discovery. During this period, the countries of Europe began to explore once more. In this time, trade routes were established or reestablished. Space was being observed again. The sciences grew both in knowledge and influence. America was "discovered." Of course, this was not necessarily a good thing if your home was one of the lands so discovered. From the perspective of the indigenous peoples, they were being invaded by those who stole their resources and their land. The Europeans also brought their Christianity with them. They self-righteously forced this religion upon the natives wherever they could. Later, they would push it upon their imported slaves. It was used to convince them that their enslavement was their natural place because it was commanded by God. It is true many Christians opposed slavery, but just as many did not. It didn't help that God seemed to miss putting "Thou shalt not enslave thy fellow man" (person) in the Ten Commandments.

One could say slavery was the first time the religious began, in a significant way, to interfere with United States society. Starting in 1863, various attempts to add God to the Constitution's preamble. These attempts were known as the Christian Amendment Movement, later the National Reform Association. The first such proposal, submitted to President Abraham Lincoln, read:

"We, the people of the United States, humbly acknowledging Almighty God as the source of all authority and power in civil government, the Lord Jesus Christ as the Ruler among the nations, His revealed will as the supreme law of the land, in order to constitute a Christian government, and in order to form a more perfect union, establish justice, insure domestic tranquility, provide for the common defense, promote the general welfare, and secure the inalienable rights and the blessings of life, liberty, and the pursuit of happiness to ourselves and our posterity, and all the people, do ordain and establish this Constitution for the United States of America."

Lincoln implied he would consider it but did not do anything further to pursue it. There would be additional attempts in 1874, 1896 and 1910 as well as in the 1940s and 1950s. None of them passed. No doubt, they will keep trying. One thing you have to say about the Christian cult, they are resilient and persistent. Even today, there are constant attempts to legislate god beliefs into the Constitution. They have often failed, but many of these do find their way into the nation's laws until someone fights back, and these laws are found to be un-Constitutional.

Beyond the many efforts to write American law, the religious (in this country, mainly Christian) have sought to influence society in other divisive and destructive ways. A favorite is to rewrite history by stating this country is a Christian nation. While this may be true technically since most US citizens would identify as Christian, the implication is the United States was founded as a Christian nation. A consulting of any descent history book will show this to be demonstrably false. If it were true, why does the Constitution not say so? Why wouldn't the Founding Fathers explain this in their writings? Why would President John Adams, a Christian himself, endorse "every clause and article thereof" a treaty (the Treaty of Tripoli, 1797), which stated in part: ...as the government of the United States of America is in not in any sense founded on the Christian Religion..." David Barton, the dubious historian whose book on

Thomas Jefferson was pulled off store shelves by his own Christian publisher for its many inaccuracies, states on his Wallbuilders website the entire text of Article 11 strengthens the Christian case. It does not. Here is the whole text quoted by Yale Law School:

"As the government of the United States of America is not in any sense founded on the Christian Religion, -as it has in itself no character of enmity against the laws, religion or tranquility of Musselmen,-and as the said States never have entered into any war or act of hostility against any Mehomitan (sic) nation, it is declared by the parties that no pretext arising from religious opinions shall ever produce an interruption of the harmony existing between the two countries."

These examples are representative of the many misrepresentations concerning our nation's history spread by the cults. You may have heard about the newest scheme to undermine our democracy. It is called Project Blitz. The brainchild of a coalition of Christian groups, Project Blitz sports a three-pronged attack to promote theocracy in the United States. 1. It sponsors legislation to distort history and allow for religious indoctrination in schools. 2. It seeks resolutions and proclamations to merge the ideas of religious freedom and history despite evidence to the contrary. 3. They also want "religious liberty protection legislation," which will allow for discrimination against homosexuals or anybody else they don't like. Again, they seek to destroy the very fabric of what this country has historically been.

Of course, history is not the only subject they attack. Since religionists hate science, particularly the theory of evolution, this is also a primary target. They flood school boards with demands to either remove Darwin or add Intelligent Design (aka Creationism) to science classes. These schemes demonstrate a fundamental ignorance of how science works. In science, the best argument wins, and that is what is taught. They think science should be a popularity contest instead of a fact-based search for truth. They don't care because they don't care for science or truth anyway.

Another outgrowth of the desire to undermine this country is the sub-cult of *Dominionism*. Dominionism is predicated on the maxim the United States should be dominated by biblical law and goals. Their doctrine calls for nothing less than the takeover of the United States. Dominionists subscribe to the seven-mountain theory. The seven mountains refer to the "mountains" of culture which they intend to supplant and dominate. They are the arts and entertainment, business, education, family, government, media, and religion. When you have lots of money and a "mission" to help the world, you naturally want to influence that world. Cults want to remake the world in their image. After all, isn't that what their god intended? They will do it despite this is contrary to the interests and ideals of this country. Now is it just me, or does this seem very much like treason?

The onslaught continues by sowing mistrust and outright hate of anyone or anything perceived as different. The tribal impulses of religion drive them to do this. Whether it is homosexuals, people of other ethnic backgrounds, women, or even those of other faiths, they seek to divide and conquer. It is the same strategy used by Donald Trump. It's no wonder they look upon him as their savior even though they claim his immoral values are abhorrent to them.

All this ultimately leads to abuse and violence. Damage, as seen from the countless cases of priests and other religious leaders who molest women and children. Not to mention the thieving televangelists and other so-called holy men and women who steal from their flocks so that they can live the lifestyles of the rich and famous. There is no need for me to document the violence of religion. You need merely to look at your newspaper or turn on the TV news. Religious violence occurs almost every day. It is very similar to the force during the reign of the Nazis, which Hitler himself declared a Christian movement. Therefore, Nazi symbols are now banned in Germany. If it can be said anything good came out of a world war, the experience began the end of religious influence on European culture. Because of the dying sway of religion in Europe, there was no need to ban it. Fortunately, or unfortunately, the United States has not had such a traumatic event of weaning our population from religion.

From practically the very moment our country came into existence, the Christians have sought to undermine it and destroy it. Even long before the time of the Founding Fathers, Christians dreamed about creating a country where their god ruled supreme. A country unburdened by any law except Biblical law, where any who didn't believe could be cast out or even better, killed.

Again, anthropologists would refer to this as tribalism. Shared beliefs form a "tribe," so any who do not share the faith are outsiders and, therefore, must be expelled from the group. It is the usual human way of acting. However, this is not the way countries should act. Countries, particularly democratic ones such as the United States, act in direct contradiction to this way of thinking. Countries, states, towns any social/political group must contradict the "normal" way of thinking. This conflict is because the political/social entities we create are intended to unite human beings. To do that, we must suppress our natural desire to keep to our own group, only be with those who share social, political, or religious beliefs, for the greater good of a harmonious society.

How, you might ask, are religious people who only want to help people and spread their faith suddenly a threat? First, they only help people *to* spread their religion. God is the be-all and end-all for everything they do in life. True, Christians build hospitals and do other work that has been good for society. The question you must ask is, *why* do they do it? While some may say it is to help people, the real reason is they believe it is to glorify their God. That sounds innocuous enough. Why should that be bad? It is terrible because of the motive. A genuine right motivation is the desire to help fellow human beings, not to glorify any god. Of course, this is the difference between religious people and Secular Humanists who think it is human beings that should be the priority, not imaginary gods made up by Bronze Age goat herders. Even so, you say, the excellent work is being done. I would say, at what cost? Think about it: all these "good" works create the perception that Christianity and religion, in general, is a beautiful thing. It is not only harmless but a powerful force for good in society. Unfortunately, we know this is not true.

Once a great believer in the separation of church and state. I defended my fellow Atheists, of course. I also supported religionists who were being attacked by other religionists. I felt everyone had a right to their beliefs so long as they didn't try to force it on others. Over my life, I have seen the religious ignore and flat out violate the First Amendment. They are brazen about it. They have made their goal quite clear. They want to rule us all. So, I suggest making religion illegal. This will, of course, require a Constitutional amendment. I know many of my fellow Atheists will bristle at this. They think freedom of speech and religion should be sacrosanct. What they need to understand is just like you cannot yell "fire" in a crowded theater, free speech should end with hate speech. At least the words that motivate people to hurt others.

In that case, beyond the fact that it is merely not true, it is used to deceive, steal from, and kill people. Those are crimes. We make other crimes illegal, such as murder, theft, using illicit drugs. Anything harmful to society. So why not religion? I have been questioned about how we can accomplish this. What I suggest is a campaign to expose religion for what it is. Expose its true nature of worship, and the people themselves demand its criminalization. The odds seem against us, but remember how the tide turned in favor of gay marriage and currently in the fight against guns with some voices suggesting we repeal the 2nd Amendment. People have also told me that if we do make religion illegal, it will merely go underground. There is some evidence for this. In Germany, Nazi and far-right groups are gaining strength this way. In this country, hate groups are doing the same, but in the open. Here is the difference; by banning Nazis and hate speech, Germany has sent a clear message Nazi views are not sanctioned by the government. Even if they cannot suppress it entirely, the people have proclaimed this is not acceptable. I realize in the United States; we value freedom of speech and freedom of religion. Still, I would argue such freedoms are dangerous when you have a large amount of uneducated populace. If we had well-educated people, they would understand that hate speech leads to hateful acts. They would also see religion as a quaint idea from our ancient past, which is useless. Ideas that are considered silly are usually harmless, but faith and hate are dangerous and can bring down a society. It is time for that to end.

R.I.P. U.S.A.

"Those who do not remember the past are
condemned to repeat it."

The oft-repeated phrase attributed to philosopher George Santayana is not just only a reminder about our past but the predictor of our likely future. What we see now in the United States is a possible slip into fascism. We have a president who admires dictators and would like to be one himself. Donald Trump is an authoritarian who has even implied he should be president for life. He thinks the country should be run as a business with him in complete control. Trump has no use for democracy or the Constitution. Therefore, he disregards the entire idea of rules, regulations, and diplomacy. Trump played on the fear and bigotry that still soils our land. He appealed to the uninformed and unintelligent, the people who want simple answers for complex problems. Trump himself is not very bright, but he does know how to manipulate people.

Trump certainly has a dictatorial state of mind. He follows the playbook of other authoritarian megalomaniacs throughout history. These include calling anyone who opposes him, enemies, undermining trust in the press and government institutions, and placing family members in government positions. Like the totalitarian regimes of the Soviet Union, China, and North Korea, Trump has demanded a military parade. A military he was too cowardly to serve in. What the hell are bone spurs anyway? In any case, we are likely to be stuck with Trump for eight years. His supporters don't know what he does and are too stupid to care. The Republicans will continue to enable Trump, and the Democrats have no candidate that can beat him since they won't run Bernie Sanders.

2016 was indeed a watershed year for the United States. It demonstrated both how stupid the electorate is and how corrupt our politicians are. This ignorance highlights my main concern. Even if we survive Trump, there is a strong probability we will not survive anyway. It appears we are following in the footprints of the Roman Empire. The signs are there. Like Rome, politics are no longer stable. There is mass corruption. The Republican Party is owned by huge banks and corporations. The Democrats are no better. Most of them are similarly held by the rich as Hilary Clinton's nomination proved. We have overexpansion of our political and economic interests and spend too much money on the military, money that could be better used at home. Our economy is in flux as the big corporations are working to appropriate all wealth for themselves. Finally, there are the cults. We have treasonous Christianity inside and barbaric Islam on the outside. They all want to destroy this country. The situation looks dire.

What comes next after the United States falls? I see two distinct possibilities. The first and least objectionable of the two is the Owners will complete their takeover of the country. In this scenario, children will only be educated enough to be able to perform their assigned tasks as predetermined by the Owners. Pay will be kept relatively low, but they will allow you to make enough to buy their products to keep the economy going. Employees will have no rights. Recently, the Supreme Court ruled workers can be required to waive their right to take part in a class-action lawsuit if they wish to gain employment. Those who do not work will simply be left to starve. The reason for their unemployment, whether it be due to injury, poor health, job elimination, or old age, will not matter. They will be considered useless eaters. As such, they do not deserve to live because they produce nothing. The concept of property will also change. You can still have small items like your clothes, your TV, and your iPad, but big-ticket items like houses and car ownership will be retained by the corporations. These things will now be rented to you. This way, when they fire you, or you displease them, they can remove you from your home as quickly as they removed you from your job. This oppression may be the stuff that brings about a revolution and creates some form of a communist dictatorship. Wouldn't that be an act of perfect revenge on the United States for Vladimir Putin? Welcome to the Corporate States of America.

Possibility number two is even worse. There will either be wars between the different religions or all-out nuclear destruction of the world. This conflict will fulfill the desire of many god-worshippers for Armageddon. If this does not occur, one religion will win dominance. Either way, this will usher in a new Dark Ages. Education will mostly become indoctrination into the cult. Philosophy and critical thinking will not be allowed. Blasphemy will become a capital offense punishable by death. The teaching of science may be made illegal. Indeed, teaching evolution will be. Innovation, both scientific and technical, will cease. Medical treatment will be reduced to praying. Sexuality will be curtailed and regulated by religious belief. Women will be oppressed, and homosexuals will be killed. Racism will become even more horrible. In the worst case, the faithful may decide to go to war to force their standards to what they see as a heathenistic world. It is most likely (but not guaranteed) Christians will win, only because this country has superior weaponry. The long-held Christian dream will be attained. Destroy the United States and impose their theocracy. Welcome to the Christian States of America.

These two factions may become embroiled in conflict with each other. As detailed in Kevin Kruse's excellent book, *One Nation Under God*, starting in the 1930s, corporations supported religious belief systems, particularly Christianity. Partly due to fear and hatred of communism and Franklin D. Roosevelt, partly to encourage American workers to be docile and productive for them. To this end, they backed religious events and causes. This strategy also included aiding some religious leaders, such as a young evangelist named Billy Graham. Graham and others not only learned how to make their congregations grow but also how to make themselves rich and gain political influence. They learned their lessons well.

Since both sides will wish to control whatever remains of the country, they will fight for dominance. The cults will want to rule by their Bible; the Owners will govern by their charter. Probably something like the fictional Ferengi Rules of Acquisition.

Can this country be saved? I don't know. This country might be too far gone to save it. The second question is, *should* this country be saved? Perhaps countries, like human beings, have a finite time on the Earth. Possibly because the United States burned so brightly, it burned itself out. The social and technical innovations this country accomplished will be enjoyed by others. It might be our destiny to be remembered in the future as the Roman Empire is remembered by us today. We did some great things, but we fell into corruption and dismay. It might be time for us to go.

Let's say this country is worth saving. We will have much to change. I do not doubt to have any chance at all; we must eliminate the influence of the Owners and the cults. This idea brings about a third possibility: revolution. Ironically, this would be a revolution to bring us back to what the Founders intended, or at least what we think they meant. While the Founders were hardly perfect, they envisioned a free country ruled first and foremost by reason. They also envisaged an educated electorate choosing leaders who would serve with honor and loyalty to the people. It is with all hope this could be accomplished peacefully in the manner in which Bernie Sanders and others subscribe. I, however, have my doubts. The religionists and the stupid have tasted power. Owners always have had an influence. None will give that power up willingly or easily. It is time for the secular, intelligent, decent people to stand up. We must do this every way we can. We must educate Americans to our real purpose of creating an honest, kind America. The one we enshrine in our ideals. We must revive the concept of honor and teach our citizens to live by it. We must once again become the light of the world.

Transforming Human Thought

Human civilization has existed for thousands of years now. We have our ways of doing things, of thinking, of being. These ways have changed due to social growth, sometimes because of things like weather, or population, catastrophe (either natural or human-made) war, scientific and technological advancement, the rise of social movements or religious cults, and so on. The changes have been slight individually, but the cumulative effect has been vast. Society constantly changes. A person from even as recently as one hundred years ago would not recognize culture as it is now.

The time for change has come once again. This time, we must change as if our lives depended on it because it does. With the quadruple threat of overpopulation, climate change, religion, and the Owners, the world is dangerously close to the end of all things. Humans must move away from their destructive paths and create a new world order.

Fortunately, we have a head start. We have Atheists and Humanists, people who aren't afraid to challenge the norm. To achieve these goals, we must do several things. We need to imitate the god-worshipers on many fronts.

Even if their intentions are terrible, they have set about realizing them in smart ways. We must do the same.

First, we must open our own Atheist and Humanist schools. I know this is something many of us desire to do. The big problem is money, as in, where do we get it? My suggestion is to ask well-heeled millionaires like Bill Gates for funding. I know that's been tried before for many good Humanist/Atheist causes but never for a school as far as I know. We could impress on Gates and others that not only will it be suitable for the purpose, but it will be a good investment as well. The schools will turn out their future executives. Students from these schools will be taught reason, logic, critical thinking skills, and the scientific method. They can learn all human knowledge. No area of study will be closed to them. The schools will cover from kindergarten to Ph.D. We will produce presidents and the masters of new industries. As soon as economically feasible, these schools will cover the entire country, eventually the world.

Second, we must become politically engaged. I don't mean working on campaigns or causes, but running for office. That has not been done very much. Why not? We are the intellectually superior, yet we let inferiors run our lives. We see what happens when religionists run things. They owe their allegiance to their cults first and their country second, if at all. Non-believer representatives would ensure truth and freedom for all because they would follow the First Amendment and the rest of the Constitution. They would take their oath of office on that hallowed document instead of the book of Bronze/Iron Age lies, the Bible.

Third, everyone has got to come out of the closet. I remember an issue of American Atheist magazine from thirty plus years ago, which depicted a traditional drawing of the sun with the caption "Everybody Out of the Closet!" This illustration was referring to Atheists who still hide their real identity from friends and family and employers. Many are celebrating Christmas and going to church. All these years later, it continues to happen. I read a Dear Abby letter (it came from my news feed) who asked if it was okay to take his children to church because his mother, who usually takes them, was going to be away for a time. My question is, why are you letting their mother take them to a church in the first place? He said in the letter he wants them to make their own choices. I've heard that often. Are you ashamed of your Atheism? Others raise their children in whatever religious tradition they have. Why shouldn't we? They can make choices when they are older. Right now, they need guidance. You know religion is wrong, so teach your children or risk losing them to a cult. If your friends and family cannot accept who you are, they don't care for you anyway. We should be out, proud and loud like the homosexual community. Look at how attitudes have changed toward gay people in the last ten years. Once vilified, LBGTs have gained acceptance throughout society. We should do the same.

True, Humanist and Atheists have made gains during this period. Our numbers have grown significantly. However, per a Pew Research article from June 1, 2016, citing the 2014 Religious Landscape Study, only one in ten Atheists share their views on Religion and God weekly with 2/3 saying they never do. This attitude must change. I'm not saying you should be going up to people on the street or knock on doors, but if someone brings up the subject, engage them, and talk about your Atheism. Most of the gains we have made are because well-known personalities like Richard Dawkins, Neil deGrasse Tyson, Bill Nye, Sam Harris, et al., have trumpeted Atheism. This trumpeting is all well and good, but I think people need to see they already know Atheists.

Atheists are members of their families, in their circle of friends, at their work, maybe even their employer. People will listen to people they know as opposed to Atheist "celebrities."

Fourth, we must show people the flaws in religion. Depending on your personality, this will take the form of anything from polite, gentle, pointing out to full-blown ridicule. You should familiarize yourself with these techniques because they will be used against you as well. God-worshipers will try to "love-bomb" you. All cults do this, from the Catholics and Protestants to the Moonies and the Hare Krishna. Failing that, they will try to denigrate and dominate you. They love to make people feel inferior because it makes them feel superior—the irony burns. You need to be able to turn this around on them and take control.

Fifth, we must campaign to see more Humanists and Atheists in mass media, particularly television. You no doubt have noticed a lack of people who think like us in the mass media. Realistically, this is a based financial decision. The powers that be do not want to offend viewers (most of whom they assume are religionists) with ideas they probably won't like. Most people do not want their preconceived notions challenged, and non-believers are the ultimate challengers.

This why neither PBS or the History Channel has never had a documentary about Humanism/Atheism. There are also very few characters in film and television that represent us as well.

That is beginning to change a little. While we always had *Star Trek*, there have been notable films about Atheists like Stephen Hawking, Alan Turing, and Steve Jobs. On television, we have seen exciting characters like Dr. Gregory House and Dr. Temperance Brennan (ironically, both on Fox.) Both are mostly positive portrayals, although both characters are a little "off." I'm sure this is partly to keep them interesting, but I also think this is done because non-believers are perceived by society as being a little "off." House was generally nasty and outright cruel despite his brilliance, while Temperance Brennan was often socially awkward and unaware. Still, *House* had an eight-year run, and *Bones* just left the air after twelve years. I wrote one lonely letter to PBS addressing the lack of non-believers; they blew me off. Start writing, particularly to PBS and the History Channel (although they seem more concerned with pawn shops, Oak Island, and truckers who drive on ice roads nowadays) and get us everywhere so people will get to know us.

Sixth, get out into your community. Do the same good work those of you who are socially inclined are doing now but let people know it is your Atheism/Humanism that drives you, not religion. Let them know it is people who must help each other because they, we, are people.

I am sure there are many more things we can do to bring Humanism and Atheism to everyone. Those who want to join us will undoubtedly be welcome. Those who do not will find themselves part of dying cults and myth.

Conclusions

We Atheists and Humanists have allowed ourselves to be pushed to the outer fringes of society when we should be running the nation. True, our numbers have been going up in recent years, but this has not kept pace with the danger we face. If we sit it out, the world may (or may not) come around. I am afraid we might not have that time to wait now we have Donald Trump as president.

I think ultimately, Trump will be a good thing for the world because he shows us what is wrong with the world. He demonstrates the worst of the joining of money and power with religion thrown into the mix. Trump has already embarrassed this country and will continue to do so. Even if he accomplishes one or two good things, the damage he does will far outweigh it. Trump is a terrible president, but he presents us with an opportunity if we have the nerve to take it.

Keith Olbermann has suggested the way to fight Trump is to continually remind him of his failures, his broken promises, and outright lies. Use every outlet available to us, especially social media. Let Trump know that even though he won the election, he is the real loser. I suggest we do the same thing to religionists and the Owners. Protest, and attack them in the media by writing letters to the editor. Attack both their political manipulations and their false beliefs too. Every time your god-worshipping friends talk about God, Jesus, or religion in general, remind them it was religionists who gave us Trump. Hammer the point home every time you can. If someone who you know voted for Trump complains to you, they have no health coverage, or their home is being taken away, remind them it is Trump and religious people who are taking it from them. Remind them churches do not pay taxes, so we must pay more. Don't give an inch, and don't be afraid. I suggest this strategy for the Owners as well.

We must make people understand religion is their enemy. We must acknowledge to ourselves religion is the enemy as well. The time for singing *Kumbaya* is passed. It is not the Sixties anymore. They have shown they do not wish to live with us but to rule us, maybe even kill us. If we can ferment mistrust of the cults, they can be defeated.

Start now. There is a Party for Reason and Progress (PORP) that hopes to bring progressive Democrats into the fold. There is also a new political action committee called 314 Action, which hopes to elect scientists to office. In New Jersey, physicist Rush Holt served in the House of Representatives for sixteen years. Scientists can win office. So can Atheists. We need to run for office and win. When we do win, we will take our oaths of office on the United States Constitution, not the Bible, as it should be.

Let us do a quick review of what our goals are. I am just listing them here. You can assign your own order of importance:

1. Transform human thought. We must teach our fellow human beings to think critically, logically, with proper respect for the scientific method. This transformation will involve a restructuring of both education and society.

2. Reduce the population. We need to reduce the population by at least two-thirds. We can do this by (A) selection of the stupid and willfully ignorant via an intelligence test. Those who do not pass will be painlessly executed or (B) give the same intelligence test with those who do not pass entered into a new Eugenics program to ensure they do not breed until they all naturally die out. I must confess I was shocked when I read a pastor suggesting the same thing I want to do, only with Muslims. I thought I might be wrong in my thinking. It was then I remembered my goal. My main concern was overpopulation and

the removal of stupid. It is not always *what* you do but *why* you do it.

3.   Stop climate change. Once the population is reduced, much of climate change will be negated. The world will naturally become less polluted because fewer people are polluting it. We will also need to enact a carbon tax and actively work on new sources of energy. We have the technology to do this right now. For the most part, it is the United States that fights against the cleaner technologies other first world countries have already implemented.

4.   Politics: Once and for all, politics must be cleaned up. Those running for office must be tested to demonstrate they know history, particularly US history, to be qualified. Voters must also submit to tests to prove they have a basic knowledge of the Constitution and understanding of the candidates and their positions to be allowed to vote. All political parties need to be disbanded. Candidates need to run on their own. All funding for campaigns must come from either a public trust fund set up for that purpose or individual citizens. All dishonest politicians must have their assets

confiscated and be executed. How about we got some of these lawyers out and put in regular citizens?

5. The economy and poverty. The reduced population will result in resources lasting longer and will allow us to replenish them. Our consumption of resources should be so far down we should be able to afford to dismantle certain aspects of our world and returning them to nature. We won't need so many houses anymore because there are far fewer people to live in them. The same can be said for shopping malls, gas (or power) stations, large cities, and so on.

We must make life better for working men and women. We must pass equal pay laws and the $15.00 (or more) minimum wage. We must improve relations between labor and management. Corporations must pay their fair of taxes as well so we can support programs that will help people and society in general.

Most importantly, we must call into account and defeat the Owners. Their greed and total disregard for humanity must be ended. They have caused suffering from almost the beginning of our civilization. It merely is not just their greed but their desire to control everything. To that end, The Owners have bought our governments wholesale. They purchased the media so they can manage that too. They genuinely want a Corporate States of America. They must be stopped; they must be punished.

6. Crime: Crime exists because we do not head off the leading causes of crime, poverty, and ignorance. Once we reduce the population, there will be less competition for resources and enough jobs for those remaining who should be competent since we have removed the stupid people. Also, we must stop repeat offenders. The most logical way to do that is to make the death penalty mandatory punishment for all crimes. I'm not talking about traffic violations (except those that cause a death) or minor crimes like low-grade shoplifting but serious crimes. I know many disapprove of the death penalty, but improved detecting techniques have reduced wrong convictions. Furthermore, those who are executed never commit another crime.

7. The media needs to police itself. In these days of rushing to get the story out first, accuracy and truthfulness are falling by the wayside. People even believe what they read on satire sites to be true. Such places should be clearly labeled as satire, or they should be considered fake news. Some of it seems to be plain laziness, some to be a desire to impose, to use Trumpspeak, "alternative facts" on the populace. Sorry Kellyanne Conway, alternative facts are just plain lies.

8. Religion must end. Depending on how we choose to reduce the population, religion will be finished quickly if we go with option A. Religionists are, of course, the willfully ignorant I spoke about earlier. If we decide option B is kinder, God-worshippers will be with us for a while. In that case, we will need to officially make religion illegal so the cultists can no longer influence our society. Perhaps an amendment to the Constitution along the lines of: "Religion, in all its forms, is now illegal in the United States. All so-called religious freedom laws are now unconstitutional." People will now be free from the evil of religion.

Once we have defeated the Owners and religionists, we can usher in a humanistic world. A world free from overpopulation, harmful climate change, war, crime, poverty, and the uneducated. Freedom of thought for all, people can love who they want to. Science and education will be at the forefront of society. Our country will be run by ordinary, well-educated people, as the Founders intended. Either we do this, or we will find ourselves in a new Dark Age. There is the choice; darkness or freedom, make your choice. Which shall it be?

Acknowledgements

There are many people I would like to acknowledge and thank for both their help and support. They deserve recognition for putting up with me all these years. However, I realize this book will be very controversial, and I do not wish anyone to experience any suffering because of me. Therefore, I will not name them, but they know who they are. I wish them all the happiness in the world.

About the Author

Jim MacIver was born in Elizabeth, NJ. He grew up in the small town of Metuchen, NJ. MacIver attended Middlesex County College and Montclair State College. He lived in Atlanta, GA, for eleven years, where he first became involved in activism. While in Georgia, he produced a cable program, *The Free Mind.* MacIver returned to NJ due to a combination of homesickness and the desire to spend time with his mother and stepfather before their deaths. He worked at several positions like Jack London. This time included a short stint at a nationwide Atheist organization.

Jim MacIver considers himself both a Secular Humanist and an Atheist. He is semi-retired, a proud uncle, and single.